BEST OF COUNTRY
Breakfast &Brunch

Rise and shine for a.m. favorites

GOOD MORNING! It'll always be a great one when you wake up with the recipes in *Best of Country Breakfast & Brunch*. This exciting new cookbook is packed with 232 easy and delicious dishes you and your family can enjoy every day of the week—from busy school mornings to weekends when you're entertaining.

In eight big chapters, you'll find a wide variety of sunny specialties sure to fit any morning's meal plan. Choose from scrumptious, quick-to-fix dishes done in 30 minutes or less…make-ahead marvels you can prepare the night before…homemade mixes that put breakfast on the fast track…and handheld foods to grab as you dash out the door.

You'll also discover down-home classics just like Mom used to make, special family favorites that are must-haves for the holidays, creatively fun foods sure to please kids and even large-yield recipes for crowds. We searched past issues of *Taste of Home* magazine and its "sister" publications to find the best daybreak dishes shared by cooks just like you.

Because every eye-opening recipe was taste-tested and approved by our Test Kitchen staff, you can rest assured that the dishes you choose will turn out right every time. Many of the recipes in this easy-to-use cookbook are shown in gorgeous full-color photos, too.

Looking for a specific type of dish? Just turn to page 108 and check the General Index, which lists recipes by food category and ingredients. Or see the Alphabetical Index to find a particular recipe.

Whether you're hosting a special-occasion brunch or just getting your family going in the morning, the sensational sunrise recipes in *Best of Country Breakfast & Brunch* will start the day off in a wholesome and delicious way!

Editor: Michelle Bretl
Art Director: Gretchen Trautman
Vice President/Books: Heidi Reuter Lloyd
Senior Editor/Books: Mark Hagen
Layout Designer: Kathy Crawford
Proofreaders: Linne Bruskewitz, Jean Steiner
Editorial Assistant: Barb Czysz
Associate Food Editors: Coleen Martin, Diane Werner
Assistant Food Editor: Karen Scales
Senior Recipe Editor: Sue A. Jurack
Recipe Editors: Mary King, Christine Rukavena

Food Photographers: Rob Hagen, Dan Roberts, Jim Wieland
Associate Photographer: Lori Foy
Food Stylist: Diane Armstrong
Set Stylists: Jennifer Bradley Vent, Stephanie Marchese
Assistant Set Stylist: Melissa Haberman
Photo Studio Coordinator: Suzanne Kern
Creative Director: Ardyth Cope
Senior Vice President/Editor in Chief: Catherine Cassidy

President: Barbara Newton
Founder: Roy Reiman

© 2007 Reiman Media Group, Inc.
5400 S. 60th St., Greendale WI 53129
International Standard Book Number (10): 0-89821-544-7
International Standard Book Number (13): 978-0-89821-544-1
Library of Congress Control Number: 2006931746
All rights reserved.
Printed in U.S.A.

Pictured on front cover: Strawberry Cheesecake French Toast (p. 8).
Pictured on back cover: Country Brunch Skillet (p. 16).

BEST OF COUNTRY
Breakfast & Brunch

Makes a Great Gift!

To order additional copies of the *Best of Country Breakfast & Brunch* book, specify item number 36575 and send $15.99 (plus $4.99 shipping/processing for one book, $5.99 for two or more) to: Country Store, Suite 9049, P.O. Box 990, Greendale WI 53129-0990. To order by credit card, call toll-free 1-800/558-1013 or visit our Web site at *www.reimanpub.com*.

Country Brunch Skillet (p. 16)

Best of Country Breakfast & Brunch

Chapter 1

Comforting Classics

Wake up to a warm, homey breakfast just like Mom used to make with these hearty eggs, golden pancakes and more.

Banana Crepes

Freda Becker, Garrettsville, Ohio

I like to serve this impressive treat on special occasions. The wonderful banana-orange flavor makes it great for breakfast, brunch and even dinner.

       2 eggs
     3/4 cup milk
       1 tablespoon butter, melted
       1 tablespoon sugar
     1/8 teaspoon salt
     1/2 cup all-purpose flour
Additional butter
ORANGE SAUCE:
     1/2 cup butter
     2/3 cup sugar
     2/3 cup orange juice
       4 teaspoons grated orange peel
       6 medium firm bananas

In a large bowl, whisk eggs, milk, melted butter, sugar and salt. Beat in flour until smooth; let stand 20 minutes.

Melt 1 teaspoon butter in an 8-in. nonstick skillet. Pour 2 tablespoons batter into the center of skillet; lift and turn pan to cover bottom. Cook until lightly browned; turn and brown the other side.

Remove to a wire rack. Repeat with remaining batter, adding butter to skillet as needed. When cool, stack crepes with waxed paper or paper towels in between.

For the orange sauce, combine butter, sugar, orange juice and orange peel in a skillet. Bring to a boil; remove from the heat. Peel bananas; cut in half lengthwise. Add to the orange sauce; cook over medium heat until heated through, about 1 minute.

Place one banana half in the center of each crepe; roll up jelly-roll style. Place folded side down on a plate; drizzle with orange sauce. **Yield:** 12 crepes.

Maple Cream Fruit Topping

Bethel Walters, Willow River, Minnesota

Transform ordinary fruit into a dessert-like delight with a dollop of this rich and creamy topping. With only five ingredients, it's a breeze to whip up just about anytime.

       1 tablespoon all-purpose flour
     3/4 cup maple syrup
       1 egg
       1 tablespoon butter
       1 cup heavy whipping cream, whipped
Assorted fresh fruit

In a saucepan, combine flour, syrup and egg until smooth. Add butter. Bring to a boil; boil and stir for 2 minutes or until thickened and bubbly.

Cover and refrigerate until completely cooled. Fold in whipped cream. Serve over fruit. **Yield:** about 2 cups.

Strawberry-Rhubarb Jam

Peggy Woodward, East Troy, Wisconsin

To me, this sweet and tangy jam tastes like summer in a jar! The fruity blend is absolutely scrumptious spread on toast, English muffins, bagels and more.

Banana Crepes

Chunky Peach Spread

water; let stand for 2 minutes. Remove peach mixture from the heat; stir in gelatin mixture until dissolved. Cool for 10 minutes. Pour into jars. Refrigerate for up to 3 weeks. **Yield:** about 3-1/2 cups.

Nutrition Facts: One serving (2 tablespoons) equals 21 calories, trace fat (0 saturated fat), 0 cholesterol, 1 mg sodium, 5 g carbohydrate, trace fiber, trace protein. **Diabetic Exchange:** 1 Free Food.

Maple Toast and Eggs

Susan Buttel, Plattsburgh, New York

My family and friends love this down-home dish each time I serve it as a morning meal. But it can also be great for lunch or dinner. The bacon, eggs and toast make these cups hearty and satisfying any time of day.

> 12 bacon strips, diced
> 1/2 cup maple syrup
> 1/4 cup butter
> 12 slices firm-textured white bread
> 12 eggs
> Salt and pepper to taste

In a large skillet, cook bacon over medium heat until crisp. Using a slotted spoon, remove to paper towels to drain. In a small saucepan, heat syrup and butter until butter is melted; set aside.

Trim the crust from the bread slices; flatten slices with a rolling pin. Brush one side of each slice generously with syrup mixture; press each slice into an ungreased muffin cup with the syrup side down. Divide the bacon among the muffin cups.

Carefully break one egg into each cup. Sprinkle with salt and pepper. Cover with foil. Bake at 400° for 18-20 minutes or until the eggs are completely cooked through. Serve immediately. **Yield:** 12 cups.

> 4 cups fresh strawberries, crushed
> 2 cups chopped fresh rhubarb
> 1/4 cup lemon juice
> 1 package (1-3/4 ounces) powdered fruit pectin
> 5-1/2 cups sugar

In a large kettle, combine the strawberries, rhubarb, lemon juice and pectin. Bring to a full rolling boil over high heat, stirring constantly. Stir in sugar; return to a full rolling boil. Boil 1 minute, stirring constantly. Remove from the heat; skim off foam.

Pour hot mixture into hot jars, leaving 1/4-in. headspace. Adjust caps. Process for 10 minutes in a boiling-water bath. **Yield:** about 6 pints.

Chunky Peach Spread

Rebecca Baird, Salt Lake City, Utah

This lovely, golden topping tastes as good as it looks! Low in sugar, it's not overly sweet...and the fresh peach flavor really comes through. You'll want to try it on everything from bagels to waffles.

✓ **Uses less fat, sugar or salt. Includes Nutrition Facts and Diabetic Exchanges.**

> 7 medium peaches (2 to 2-1/2 pounds)
> 1/3 cup sugar
> 1 tablespoon lemon juice
> 1 envelope unflavored gelatin
> 1/4 cup cold water

Drop the peaches in boiling water for 1 minute or until the peel has softened. Immediately dip peaches in ice water. Peel and chop peaches. In a large saucepan, combine the peaches, sugar and lemon juice. Bring to a boil. Mash peaches. Reduce heat; simmer, uncovered, for 5 minutes.

Meanwhile, in a small bowl, sprinkle gelatin over cold

Maple Toast and Eggs

Blueberry Breakfast Sauce

Strawberry Cheesecake French Toast

(Pictured on front cover)

Darlene Brenden, Salem, Oregon

For a tempting breakfast dish that's almost like dessert, try this! The rich and creamy filling between the slices of French toast tastes just like cheesecake.

- 1 carton (8 ounces) ricotta cheese
- 3 tablespoons confectioners' sugar
- 1 teaspoon vanilla extract
- 16 slices French bread (1/2 inch thick)
- 2 eggs
- 1 cup milk
- 2 cups sliced fresh *or* frozen strawberries

Maple syrup and additional confectioners' sugar

In a small bowl, combine ricotta, sugar and vanilla. Spread 2 tablespoons on each of eight slices of bread; top with remaining bread. In a bowl, beat eggs and milk; soak sandwiches for 1-2 minutes per side.

Cook on a greased hot griddle for 5 minutes on each side or until golden brown and heated through. Serve with strawberries. Top with syrup and additional confectioners' sugar. **Yield:** 4-6 servings.

Blueberry Breakfast Sauce

Ellen Benninger, Stoneboro, Pennsylvania

Bursting with blueberries, this topping is great served over pancakes, French toast, waffles or even ice cream. Whether you use fresh or frozen berries, the flavor is fantastic...and with only four ingredients, it cooks up in a flash.

- 1/2 cup sugar
- 1 tablespoon cornstarch
- 1/3 cup water
- 2 cups fresh *or* frozen blueberries

In a 2-qt. saucepan, combine sugar and cornstarch; gradually stir in water. Add blueberries; bring to a boil over medium heat, stirring constantly. Boil for 1 minute, stirring occasionally. Serve blueberry sauce warm or cold over French toast, pancakes or waffles. **Yield:** about 2 cups.

Spinach Cheese Strata

Mary Laffey, Indianapolis, Indiana

Here's the perfect brunch bake for the holidays. Sometimes I garnish it with red and green pepper rings in the center.

- 1/2 cup chopped onion
- 1/4 cup chopped sweet red pepper
- 1/4 cup chopped green pepper
- 2 tablespoons butter
- 1 package (10 ounces) frozen chopped spinach, thawed and well drained
- 2 cups Wheat Chex

Cran-Strawberry Cooler

Clara Coulston, Washington Court House, Ohio

This frothy refresher blends strawberries with cranberry juice, white grape juice and ice. It's a beverage that hits the spot wherever you serve it.

- 1-1/3 cups cranberry juice
- 2/3 cup white grape juice
- 9 to 10 fresh strawberries, *divided*
- 4 ice cubes
- 1/2 to 1 teaspoon sugar, optional

In a blender, combine the juices, six strawberries, ice and sugar if desired. Cover and process until smooth. Pour into glasses. Garnish with remaining strawberries. **Yield:** 3-4 servings.

Spinach Cheese Strata

1/2 cup shredded cheddar cheese
1/2 cup shredded Swiss cheese
  6 eggs
  2 cups milk
1/3 cup crumbled cooked bacon
  1 teaspoon Dijon mustard
  1 teaspoon salt
1/4 teaspoon white pepper

In a skillet, saute the onion and peppers in butter until crisp-tender. Remove from the heat.

Add spinach and cereal; mix well. Spoon into a greased 11-in. x 7-in. x 2-in. baking dish. Sprinkle with cheese. In a bowl, combine the eggs, milk, bacon, mustard, salt and pepper. Pour over cheese. Bake at 325° for 45-50 minutes or until a knife inserted near the center comes out clean. Let stand for 10 minutes before cutting. **Yield:** 6-8 servings.

Black Forest Waffles

Swiss Cheese Potato Pancakes

Ferne Moe, Northbrook, Illinois

When I was searching for just the right side dish to perk up a meal, my neighbor suggested these pancakes. Golden brown, crisp and cheesy, they did the trick!

  1 package (3 ounces) cream cheese, softened
  2 eggs
  2 tablespoons all-purpose flour
  4 cups shredded peeled potatoes
    (about 1 pound)
1/4 cup shredded Swiss cheese
  2 tablespoons grated onion
1/4 teaspoon salt
1/8 teaspoon pepper
Dash cayenne pepper
  3 tablespoons butter
  3 tablespoons vegetable oil

In a mixing bowl, beat cream cheese until smooth. Add eggs, one at a time, beating well after each addition. Add flour; mix well. Stir in potatoes, Swiss cheese, onion, salt, pepper and cayenne pepper.

In a large skillet, heat butter and oil over medium heat. Drop batter by 1/4 cupfuls; press lightly to flatten. Fry until golden and crisp, about 5 minutes on each side. Drain on paper towels. **Yield:** 16 pancakes.

Black Forest Waffles

Edith Johnson, Fruita, Colorado

With their dark chocolate flavor and topping of cherries and whipped cream, these made-from-scratch waffles add an extra-special touch to brunch with very little effort.

1-3/4 cups cake flour
  6 tablespoons sugar
  1 tablespoon baking powder
1/2 teaspoon salt
  2 eggs, *separated*
  1 cup milk
  2 squares (1 ounce *each*) unsweetened
    baking chocolate
  3 tablespoons shortening
  1 cup heavy whipping cream, whipped
  3 tablespoons confectioners' sugar
  1 can (21 ounces) cherry pie filling
Fresh mint, optional

In a mixing bowl, combine flour, sugar, baking powder and salt. Combine egg yolks and milk; stir into dry ingredients. In a double boiler or microwave, melt the chocolate and shortening. Add to batter; mix well. In another mixing bowl, beat egg whites until stiff peaks form; fold into the batter.

Bake in a preheated waffle iron according to manufacturer's directions until browned. Combine whipped cream and confectioners' sugar. Serve waffles topped with whipped cream and pie filling. Garnish with mint if desired. **Yield:** 5 waffles (about 6-3/4 inches).

Tempting Toppings

Try accenting the chocolaty waffles on this page with raspberry pie filling instead of cherry. Can't get enough chocolate? Sprinkle on some mini chocolate chips!

Orange-Cinnamon French Toast

Orange-Cinnamon French Toast

Bernice Smith, Sturgeon Lake, Minnesota

This yummy toast is oven-baked, so all of the slices are ready at once...and everyone can dig in at the same time.

☑ **Uses less fat, sugar or salt. Includes Nutrition Facts and Diabetic Exchanges.**

  2 to 4 tablespoons butter, melted
  2 tablespoons honey
1/2 teaspoon ground cinnamon
  3 eggs
1/2 cup orange juice
1/8 teaspoon salt, optional
  6 slices bread
Additional honey, optional

In a bowl, combine butter, honey and cinnamon. Pour into a greased 13-in. x 9-in. x 2-in. baking pan; spread to coat bottom of pan. In a shallow bowl, beat eggs, orange juice and salt if desired. Dip bread into egg mixture and place in prepared pan.

  Bake at 400° for 15-20 minutes or until golden brown. Invert onto a serving platter; serve with honey if desired. **Yield:** 6 slices.

  Nutrition Facts: One slice (prepared with 2 tablespoons reduced-fat margarine, egg substitute equivalent to 3 eggs, and without salt and additional honey) equals 158 calories, 5 g fat (0 saturated fat), 1 mg cholesterol, 231 mg sodium, 23 g carbohydrate, 0 fiber, 6 g protein. **Diabetic Exchanges:** 1-1/2 starch, 1 fat.

Citrus Grape Drink

Sylvia Murphy, River Ranch, Florida

My mom made this tangy, refreshing beverage often while I was growing up, and I loved it. When I got married, I requested that it be served at our wedding reception.

  4 cups water
  1 cup sugar
  2 cups red grape juice, chilled
1/3 cup lemon juice, chilled
1/3 cup orange juice, chilled

In a saucepan, heat the water and sugar until the sugar is dissolved. Cool. Pour into a large pitcher or punch bowl; stir in the fruit juices. Serve over ice. **Yield:** about 2 quarts.

Crispy Baked Oatmeal

Shirley Martin, Ephrata, Pennsylvania

This fresh-from-the-oven cereal is a favorite in my family, especially on cool fall and winter days. With cinnamon, raisins, coconut and chocolate chips, the mixture is sure to be popular with your family, too.

  2 eggs
1/2 cup vegetable oil
1/3 cup packed brown sugar
  3 cups old-fashioned oats
  3 teaspoons baking powder
  1 teaspoon salt
3/4 teaspoon ground cinnamon
1/3 cup flaked coconut
1/3 cup raisins
1/3 cup semisweet chocolate chips
Milk, optional

In a bowl, combine eggs, oil and brown sugar. Combine the oats, baking powder, salt and cinnamon; add to egg mixture, stirring just until moistened. Stir in the coconut, raisins and chocolate chips.

  Spoon into a greased 13-in. x 9-in. x 2-in. baking dish. Bake, uncovered, at 350° for 20-25 minutes or until edges are golden brown. Serve warm with milk if desired. **Yield:** 4 servings.

Baked Canadian-Style Bacon

Myra Innes, Auburn, Kansas

Brown sugar, pineapple juice and ground mustard nicely season these slices of Canadian bacon. They take just moments to prepare, and you can easily double the recipe when entertaining a crowd.

  1 pound sliced Canadian bacon
1/4 cup packed brown sugar
1/4 cup pineapple juice
1/4 teaspoon ground mustard

Place the bacon in a greased 11-in. x 7-in. x 2-in. baking dish. In a bowl, combine the brown sugar, pineapple juice and mustard. Pour over the bacon. Cover and bake at 325° for 25-30 minutes or until heated through. **Yield:** 6-8 servings.

Deluxe Ham Omelet

Iola Egle, Bella Vista, Arkansas

Ham, a variety of vegetables and two cheeses make this omelet truly "deluxe." It's a hearty meal for one or two.

        3 eggs
        2 tablespoons half-and-half cream
        2 tablespoons minced chives
    1/2 teaspoon garlic salt
    1/4 teaspoon pepper
        1 tablespoon olive oil
    1/2 cup finely chopped fully cooked ham
        2 tablespoons chopped green pepper
        2 tablespoons chopped tomato
        2 fresh mushrooms, sliced
        2 tablespoons shredded cheddar cheese
        2 tablespoons shredded part-skim mozzarella
          cheese

In a small bowl, beat the eggs, cream, chives, garlic salt and pepper. Heat oil in a large skillet over medium heat; add egg mixture. As eggs set, lift edges, letting uncooked portion flow underneath.

When the eggs are set, spoon ham, green pepper, tomato, mushrooms and cheeses over one side; fold omelet over filling. Cover and let stand for 1-1/2 minutes or until cheese is melted. **Yield:** 1-2 servings.

Hash Brown Potatoes

Holly Jean VeDepo, West Liberty, Iowa

My mother-in-law served these buttery potatoes at brunch a while ago, and I couldn't leave without requesting the recipe. Chopped red pepper provides this stovetop side dish with a bit of color.

        4 medium baking potatoes
    1/4 cup finely chopped onion
    1/2 medium sweet red pepper, cut into
          1-inch strips, optional
        2 tablespoons all-purpose flour
    1/4 cup milk
    1/4 teaspoon salt
Pepper to taste
    1/4 cup butter

Pierce the potatoes; place on a microwave-safe plate. Microwave, uncovered, on high for 12-14 minutes or until tender, turning once. Cool slightly; peel and cube.

Place potatoes in a bowl; add onion and red pepper if desired. In another bowl, combine the flour, milk, salt and pepper until smooth. Pour over potato mixture and toss.

In a large skillet, melt butter. Add potato mixture. Cook over medium heat for 15 minutes or until potatoes are golden brown, stirring occasionally. **Yield:** 6 servings.

Deluxe Ham Omelet

Caramelized Bacon Twists

Caramelized Bacon Twists

Jane Paschke, Duluth, Minnesota

A friend gave me this recipe to use for a bridal shower brunch, and the sweet, chewy bacon strips got rave reviews. Lining the pan with aluminum foil before baking helps cut down on cleanup.

> 1 pound sliced bacon
> 1/2 cup packed brown sugar
> 2 teaspoons ground cinnamon

Cut each bacon strip in half widthwise. Combine the brown sugar and cinnamon. Dip the bacon strips in the sugar mixture; twist.

Place on a foil-lined 15-in. x 10-in. x 1-in. baking pan. Bake at 350° for 15-20 minutes or until crisp. Serve; or cool and freeze in an airtight container for up to 1 month. **Yield:** 3 dozen.

Maple Pancakes

Mary Colbath, Concord, New Hampshire

Our family always looks forward to tapping maple trees in March...and then enjoying the pure syrup year-round. This recipe is one of my favorite ways to use that syrup.

> 1 cup all-purpose flour
> 1-1/2 teaspoons baking powder
> 1/2 teaspoon salt
> 1 egg
> 1 cup milk
> 2 tablespoons vegetable oil
> 1 tablespoon maple syrup

In a bowl, combine flour, baking powder and salt. In another bowl, combine egg, milk, oil and syrup; stir into dry ingredients just until blended.

Pour batter by 1/4 cupfuls onto a lightly greased hot griddle; turn when bubbles form on top of pancakes. Cook until second side is golden brown (pancakes will be thin). **Yield:** 6-7 pancakes.

Danish Twists

Charys Rockey, Rochelle, Texas

My twin sister and I love to bake together, and this was one of the first yeast breads we tried. Any day becomes a special occasion when these buttery twists are on the menu!

> 2 packages (1/4 ounce *each*) active dry yeast
> 1-1/2 cups warm milk (110° to 115°)
> 4 cups all-purpose flour
> 1/2 cup sugar
> 2 teaspoons salt
> 1 cup cold butter
> 4 egg yolks, beaten
> 2 egg whites, beaten
> Seedless raspberry jam *or* apricot preserves
> GLAZE:
> 1-1/2 cups confectioners' sugar
> 3/4 teaspoon vanilla extract
> 2 to 3 tablespoons milk

In a bowl, dissolve yeast in warm milk. In a large bowl, combine the flour, sugar and salt. Using a pastry blender, cut in butter until crumbly. Stir in yeast mixture and egg yolks. Cover and refrigerate overnight.

Punch dough down. Turn onto a lightly floured surface; divide into thirds. Roll each portion into a 9-in. x 7-in. rectangle. Cut into 7-in. x 1-in. strips. Pinch ends together, forming a circle; twist once to form a figure eight. Place 2 in. apart on greased baking sheets. Cover and let rise until doubled, about 20 minutes.

Brush with egg whites. Make an indentation in the center of each loop; fill with jam. Bake at 350° for 14-16 minutes or until golden brown. Remove from pans to wire racks. In a small bowl, combine glaze ingredients. Drizzle over warm rolls. **Yield:** 27 rolls.

Sausage and Egg Casserole

Gayle Grigg, Phoenix, Arizona

For the perfect combination of eggs, sausage, bread and cheese, try this dish. My mom and I like it because it bakes up tender and golden, slices beautifully and goes over well whenever we serve it.

> 1 pound bulk pork sausage
> 6 eggs
> 2 cups milk
> 1 teaspoon salt
> 1 teaspoon ground mustard
> 6 slices white bread, cut into 1/2-inch cubes
> 1 cup (4 ounces) shredded cheddar cheese

In a skillet, brown and crumble sausage; drain and set aside. In a large bowl, beat eggs; add milk, salt and mustard. Stir in bread cubes, cheese and sausage.

Pour into a greased 11-in. x 7-in. x 2-in. baking dish. Cover and refrigerate for 8 hours or overnight. Remove from the refrigerator 30 minutes before baking. Bake, uncovered, at 350° for 40 minutes or until a knife inserted near the center comes out clean. Let stand for 10 minutes before slicing. **Yield:** 8-10 servings.

Caramel-Pecan Sticky Buns

Judy Powell, Star, Idaho

My mother used to bake delicious cinnamon rolls when I was a child. Later, she taught my sister and me to make them. I've since added the caramel and pecans.

       1 **package (1/4 ounce) active dry yeast**
    3/4 **cup warm water (110° to 115°)**
    3/4 **cup warm milk (110° to 115°)**
    1/4 **cup sugar**
       3 **tablespoons vegetable oil**
       2 **teaspoons salt**
 3-3/4 to 4-1/4 **cups all-purpose flour**
FILLING:
    1/4 **cup butter, softened**
    1/4 **cup sugar**
       3 **teaspoons ground cinnamon**
    3/4 **cup packed brown sugar**
    1/2 **cup heavy whipping cream**
       1 **cup coarsely chopped pecans**

In a large mixing bowl, dissolve yeast in warm water. Add the milk, sugar, oil, salt and 1-1/4 cups flour. Beat on medium speed for 2-3 minutes or until smooth. Stir in enough remaining flour to form a soft dough.

Turn onto a floured surface; knead until smooth and elastic, about 6-8 minutes. Place in a greased bowl, turning once to grease top. Cover and let rise in a warm place until doubled, about 1 hour.

Caramel-Pecan Sticky Buns

Poppy Seed Mini Muffins

Punch dough down. Turn onto a lightly floured surface. Roll into an 18-in. x 12-in. rectangle. Spread butter to within 1/2 in. of edges. Combine sugar and cinnamon; sprinkle over butter. Roll up jelly-roll style, starting with a long side; pinch seam to seal. Cut roll into 12 slices.

Combine brown sugar and cream; pour into a greased 13-in. x 9-in. x 2-in. baking pan. Sprinkle with pecans. Place rolls cut side down over pecans. Cover and let rise until doubled, about 1 hour.

Bake at 350° for 30-35 minutes or until well browned. Cool for 1 minute before inverting onto a serving platter. **Yield:** 1 dozen.

Poppy Seed Mini Muffins

Kathryn Anderson, Casper, Wyoming

These moist goodies may be small, but they're a big hit on a buffet, as a snack or even inside a brown-bag lunch.

       2 **cups all-purpose flour**
    3/4 **cup sugar**
       1 **teaspoon baking powder**
       1 **teaspoon baking soda**
    1/4 **teaspoon salt**
       1 **cup (8 ounces) sour cream**
    1/2 **cup vegetable oil**
       2 **eggs**
       2 **tablespoons poppy seeds**
       2 **tablespoons milk**
    1/2 **teaspoon vanilla extract**
    1/2 **teaspoon lemon extract**

In a large bowl, combine flour, sugar, baking powder, baking soda and salt; set aside. Combine remaining ingredients; mix well. Stir into dry ingredients just until moistened.

Fill greased or paper-lined mini-muffin cups two-thirds full. Bake at 400° for 12-15 minutes or until a toothpick comes out clean. Cool in pan 10 minutes before removing to a wire rack. **Yield:** about 3-1/2 dozen.

Gran's Granola Parfaits

Angela Keller, Newburgh, Indiana

When my mother-in-law ("Gran" to our children) had us over for brunch, we really enjoyed her fancy yogurt parfaits. They were refreshing, light and wholesome. I experimented a bit with her recipe and came up with this sweet and nutty variation. Yum!

  2 cups old-fashioned oats
  1 cup Wheaties
  1 cup whole almonds
  1 cup pecan halves
  1 cup flaked coconut
4-1/2 teaspoons wheat germ
  1 tablespoon sesame seeds, toasted
  1 teaspoon ground cinnamon
1/4 cup butter, melted
  2 tablespoons maple syrup
  2 tablespoons honey
  1 can (20 ounces) pineapple tidbits, drained
  1 can (15 ounces) mandarin oranges, drained
  1 cup halved green grapes
  2 to 3 medium firm bananas, sliced
  1 cup sliced fresh strawberries
  1 carton (32 ounces) vanilla yogurt

In a bowl, combine the first eight ingredients. Combine the butter, syrup and honey; drizzle over oat mixture and stir until well coated. Pour into a greased 13-in. x 9-in. x 2-in. baking pan. Bake, uncovered, at 350° for 30 minutes, stirring every 10 minutes. Cool on a wire rack; crumble into pieces.

Combine the fruits in a large bowl. For each parfait, layer 2 tablespoons yogurt, 2 tablespoons granola and 3 round tablespoons fruit in a parfait glass or dessert bowl. Repeat layers. Sprinkle with remaining granola. Serve immediately. **Yield:** 16 servings.

Gran's Granola Parfaits

Raspberry Crumb Cake

Raspberry Crumb Cake

Pat Habiger, Spearville, Kansas

With a spiced crust, tangy raspberry filling and crunchy almond topping, this coffee cake will brighten any buffet. Its homemade taste brings folks back for seconds.

2/3 cup sugar
1/4 cup cornstarch
3/4 cup water
  2 cups fresh *or* frozen unsweetened raspberries
  1 tablespoon lemon juice
CRUST:
  3 cups all-purpose flour
  1 cup sugar
  1 tablespoon baking powder
  1 teaspoon salt
  1 teaspoon ground cinnamon
1/4 teaspoon ground mace
  1 cup cold butter
  2 eggs
  1 cup milk
  1 teaspoon vanilla extract
TOPPING:
1/2 cup all-purpose flour
1/2 cup sugar
1/4 cup cold butter
1/4 cup sliced almonds

In a saucepan, combine sugar, cornstarch, water and raspberries. Bring to a boil over medium heat; boil for 5 minutes or until thickened, stirring constantly. Remove from the heat; stir in lemon juice. Cool.

Meanwhile, in a bowl, combine the first six crust ingredients. Cut in butter until mixture resembles coarse crumbs. Beat eggs, milk and vanilla; add to crumb mixture and mix well. Spread two-thirds of the mixture into a greased 13-in. x 9-in. x 2-in. baking dish. Spoon raspberry filling over crust to within 1 in. of the edges. Top with remaining crust mixture.

For topping, combine flour and sugar; cut in butter until crumbly. Stir in almonds. Sprinkle over the top. Bake at 350° for 50-55 minutes or until lightly browned. **Yield:** 12-16 servings.

Touch of Spring Muffins

Gail Sykora, Menomonee Falls, Wisconsin

Strawberries and rhubarb are a winning combination, and the sweet-tart flavor makes these muffins absolutely delightful. Remember this recipe when your backyard rhubarb is ready to cut or you see fresh stalks at the store.

      2 cups all-purpose flour
    1/2 cup sugar
      1 tablespoon baking powder
    1/2 teaspoon salt
      1 egg
    3/4 cup milk
    1/3 cup vegetable oil
    1/2 cup sliced fresh strawberries
    1/2 cup sliced fresh rhubarb
TOPPING:
      6 small fresh strawberries, halved
      2 teaspoons sugar

In a large bowl, combine flour, sugar, baking powder and salt. In another bowl, beat egg, milk and oil until smooth. Stir into dry ingredients just until moistened. Fold in strawberries and rhubarb.

Fill greased or paper-lined muffin cups three-fourths full. Place a strawberry half, cut side down, on each. Sprinkle with sugar. Bake at 375° for 22-25 minutes or until a toothpick comes out clean. Cool for 5 minutes before removing from pan to a wire rack. Serve warm. **Yield:** 1 dozen.

Spiced Coffee with Cream

Alpha Wilson, Roswell, New Mexico

I discovered this recipe many years ago, and we've enjoyed it countless times since. The special coffee is perfect for company, but I've also made it as a treat for my husband and me on leisurely weekend mornings.

    1/4 cup evaporated milk
  2-1/4 teaspoons confectioners' sugar
    1/4 teaspoon ground cinnamon
    1/8 teaspoon vanilla extract
      1 cup hot strong brewed coffee
Ground nutmeg
      2 cinnamon sticks

Pour milk into a small mixing bowl; place mixer beaters in the bowl. Cover and freeze for 30 minutes or until ice crystals begin to form.

Add the sugar, cinnamon and vanilla; beat until thick and fluffy. Pour about 1/2 cup into each cup. Add coffee; sprinkle with nutmeg. Serve immediately; garnish with cinnamon sticks if desired. **Yield:** 2 servings.

Blintz Pancakes

Dianna Digoy, San Diego, California

Blending sour cream and cottage cheese into the batter of these pancakes gives them their traditional blintz flavor. Top these family favorites with berry syrup, and you'll turn an ordinary morning into an extraordinary one!

☑ **Uses less fat, sugar or salt. Includes Nutrition Facts and Diabetic Exchanges.**

      1 cup all-purpose flour
      1 tablespoon sugar
    1/2 teaspoon salt
      1 cup (8 ounces) sour cream
      1 cup (8 ounces) small-curd cottage cheese
      4 eggs, lightly beaten
Strawberry *or* blueberry syrup, optional
Sliced fresh strawberries, optional

In a bowl, combine the flour, sugar and salt; mix well. Add the sour cream, cottage cheese and eggs; mix just until combined.

Spoon 1/4 cupfuls of batter onto a greased hot griddle. Turn when edges are set; cook until the second side is golden brown. Serve with syrup and strawberries if desired. **Yield:** 12 pancakes.

Nutrition Facts: Two pancakes (prepared with reduced-fat sour cream, fat-free cottage cheese and 1 cup egg substitute; calculated without syrup or strawberries) equals 184 calories, 4 g fat (3 g saturated fat), 17 mg cholesterol, 429 mg sodium, 23 g carbohydrate, 1 g fiber, 14 g protein. **Diabetic Exchanges:** 1-1/2 starch, 1 lean meat.

Blintz Pancakes

Raisin Banana Bread

Margaret Hinman, Burlington, Iowa

Grated carrots, zucchini, raisins and nuts bring a wonderful blend of flavors to this out-of-the-ordinary banana bread.

- 3 cups all-purpose flour
- 2 cups sugar
- 1 teaspoon baking powder
- 1 teaspoon salt
- 1 teaspoon pumpkin pie spice
- 1/2 teaspoon baking soda
- 1/2 teaspoon ground cinnamon
- 3 eggs
- 1 cup vegetable oil
- 2 teaspoons vanilla extract
- 1 cup grated zucchini
- 1 cup grated carrot
- 1/2 cup mashed ripe banana
- 1/2 cup raisins
- 1/2 cup chopped walnuts

In a mixing bowl, combine the first seven ingredients. Add eggs, oil and vanilla; mix well. Stir in zucchini, carrot, banana, raisins and nuts.

Pour into four greased and floured 5-3/4-in. x 3-in. x 2-in. loaf pans. Bake at 350° for 45-48 minutes or until a toothpick inserted near the center comes out clean. Cool for 10 minutes; remove from pans to wire racks. **Yield:** 4 loaves.

Country Brunch Skillet

(Pictured on page 4 and back cover)

Elvira Brunnquell, Port Washington, Wisconsin

Frozen hash brown potatoes and packaged shredded cheese cut down the preparation time for this hearty breakfast...and the sight of this home-style skillet cooking on the stove is a surefire eye-opener!

- 6 bacon strips
- 6 cups frozen cubed hash brown potatoes
- 3/4 cup chopped green pepper
- 1/2 cup chopped onion
- 1 teaspoon salt
- 1/4 teaspoon pepper
- 6 eggs
- 1/2 cup shredded cheddar cheese

In a large skillet over medium heat, cook bacon until crisp. Remove bacon; crumble and set aside. Drain, reserving 2 tablespoons of drippings. Add potatoes, green pepper, onion, salt and pepper to drippings; cook and stir for 2 minutes. Cover and cook, stirring occasionally, until potatoes are browned and tender, about 15 minutes.

Make six wells in the potato mixture; break one egg into each well. Cover and cook on low heat for 8-10 minutes or until eggs are completely set. Sprinkle with cheese and bacon. **Yield:** 6 servings.

Apple Fritter Rings

Bernice Snowberger, Monticello, Indiana

This is an old-fashioned treat that folks of all ages enjoy. Sprinkled with sugar and cinnamon, the warm fritters are finger-licking good.

    1 egg
  2/3 cup milk
    1 teaspoon vegetable oil
    1 cup all-purpose flour
    2 tablespoons sugar
    1 teaspoon baking powder
Dash salt
    5 large tart apples
1-1/2 cups vegetable oil
  1/4 cup sugar
  1/2 teaspoon ground cinnamon

In a bowl, beat egg, milk and oil. Combine flour, sugar, baking powder and salt; stir into the egg mixture until smooth (batter will be thick). Peel, core and cut apples into 1/2-in. rings.

In an electric skillet or deep-fat fryer, heat oil to 375°. Dip apple rings into batter; fry, a few at a time, until golden brown. Drain on paper towels. Combine sugar and cinnamon; sprinkle over hot fritters. Serve warm. **Yield:** about 2 dozen.

Homemade Sage Sausage Patties

Diane Hixon, Niceville, Florida

Oregano, garlic and sage add zippy flavor to these quick-to-fix ground pork patties. I've had this Pennsylvania Dutch recipe for years, and it always gets compliments.

  3/4 cup shredded cheddar cheese
  1/4 cup buttermilk

Homemade Sage Sausage Patties

Morning Orange Drink

    1 tablespoon finely chopped onion
    2 teaspoons rubbed sage
  3/4 teaspoon salt
  3/4 teaspoon pepper
  1/8 teaspoon garlic powder
  1/8 teaspoon dried oregano
    1 pound ground pork

In a bowl, combine the first eight ingredients. Crumble pork over mixture and mix well. Shape into eight 1/2-in. patties. Refrigerate for 1 hour.

In a nonstick skillet over medium heat, fry patties for 6-8 minutes on each side or until meat is no longer pink. **Yield:** 8 servings.

Morning Orange Drink

Joyce Mummau, Mt. Airy, Maryland

This breakfast beverage requires just a few basic ingredients and little preparation. It draws raves from overnight guests about its "wake-you-up" taste.

    1 can (6 ounces) frozen orange juice
       concentrate
    1 cup cold water
    1 cup milk
  1/3 cup sugar
    1 teaspoon vanilla extract
   10 ice cubes

Combine the first five ingredients in a blender; process at high speed. Add ice cubes, a few at a time, blending until smooth. Serve immediately. **Yield:** 4-6 servings.

Ham 'n' Cheese Quiche

Ham 'n' Cheese Quiche

Christena Palmer, Green River, Wyoming

When I was pregnant with our daughter, I made and froze some of these cheesy quiches. After her birth, it was nice to have a homemade, ready-to-bake meal in the freezer when my husband and I were too tired to cook.

- 2 pastry shells (9 inches)
- 2 cups diced fully cooked ham
- 2 cups (8 ounces) shredded sharp cheddar cheese
- 2 teaspoons dried minced onion
- 4 eggs
- 2 cups half-and-half cream
- 1/2 teaspoon salt
- 1/4 teaspoon pepper

Line unpricked pastry shells with a double thickness of heavy-duty foil. Bake at 400° for 5 minutes. Remove foil; bake 5 minutes longer.

Divide ham, cheese and onion between the shells. In a bowl, whisk eggs, cream, salt and pepper. Pour into shells. Cover and freeze for up to 3 months. Or cover edges with foil and bake at 400° for 35-40 minutes or until a knife inserted near the center comes out clean. Let stand for 5-10 minutes before cutting. **Yield:** 2 quiches (6 servings each).

Fluffy Waffles

Amy Gilles, Ellsworth, Wisconsin

A friend shared the recipe for these light and delicious waffles. The accompanying cinnamon syrup is a nice change from the usual maple syrup, and it keeps quite well in the fridge. Our two children also like it on toast.

- 2 cups all-purpose flour
- 1 tablespoon sugar
- 2 teaspoons baking powder
- 1/2 teaspoon salt
- 3 eggs, *separated*
- 2 cups milk
- 1/4 cup vegetable oil

CINNAMON CREAM SYRUP:
- 1 cup sugar
- 1/2 cup light corn syrup
- 1/4 cup water
- 1 can (5 ounces) evaporated milk
- 1 teaspoon vanilla extract
- 1/2 teaspoon ground cinnamon

In a bowl, combine the flour, sugar, baking powder and salt. Combine the egg yolks, milk and oil; stir into dry ingredients just until moistened. In a small mixing bowl, beat egg whites until stiff peaks form; fold into batter. Bake in a preheated waffle iron according to manufacturer's directions.

Meanwhile, for syrup, combine sugar, corn syrup and water in a saucepan. Bring to a boil over medium heat; cook and stir for 2 minutes or until thickened. Remove from the heat; stir in the milk, vanilla and cinnamon. Serve with waffles. **Yield:** 8-10 waffles (6-1/2 inches) and 1-2/3 cups syrup.

Rolled Swedish Pancakes

Tami Escher, Dumont, Minnesota

There's a heavenly hint of lemon wrapped inside these rich, flavorful pancakes. They make breakfast extra-special and don't take long to prepare.

- 1/2 cup plus 1 tablespoon sugar, *divided*
- 2 tablespoons grated lemon peel
- 1-1/2 cups all-purpose flour
- 1/2 teaspoon salt
- 8 eggs
- 3 cups milk
- 3 tablespoons butter, melted

Sour cream and cherry preserves

Combine 1/2 cup sugar and the lemon peel; set aside. In a bowl, combine the flour, salt and remaining sugar. Beat the eggs, milk and butter; stir into the dry ingredients and mix well.

Pour batter by 1/2 cupfuls onto a lightly greased hot griddle; cook until set and lightly browned. Turn; cook

1 minute longer. Immediately sprinkle each pancake with lemon-sugar mixture; roll up and keep warm. Top with sour cream and preserves. **Yield:** 1 dozen.

Sour Cream Peach Kuchen

Cathy Elands, Hightstown, New Jersey

For an old-fashioned breakfast treat, nothing beats my mother's peach kuchen. I love the tender crust, lightly sweet filling and sour cream topping.

      3 cups all-purpose flour
1-1/4 cups sugar, *divided*
  1/2 teaspoon baking powder
  1/4 teaspoon salt
      1 cup cold butter
      2 cans (29 ounces *each*) sliced peaches, drained *or* 13 small fresh peaches, peeled and sliced
      1 teaspoon ground cinnamon
TOPPING:
      4 egg yolks
      2 cups (16 ounces) sour cream
      2 to 3 tablespoons sugar
  1/4 teaspoon ground cinnamon

In a bowl, combine the flour, 1/4 cup sugar, baking powder and salt; cut in the butter until the mixture resembles coarse crumbs. Press onto the bottom and 1 in. up the sides of a greased 13-in. x 9-in. x 2-in. baking dish. Arrange the peaches over the crust. Combine the cinnamon and remaining sugar; sprinkle over the peach-

French Toast Custard

es. Bake at 400° for 15 minutes.

Meanwhile, in a bowl, combine egg yolks and sour cream. Spread evenly over peaches. Combine sugar and cinnamon; sprinkle over top. Bake 30-35 minutes longer or until golden brown. Serve warm or cold. Store leftovers in the refrigerator. **Yield:** 12 servings.

French Toast Custard

Pamela Hamp, Arroyo Grande, California

I usually prepare this dish for brunch, but it's terrific any time at all. Everyone says it just melts in your mouth.

      8 to 10 slices day-old French bread (1 inch thick)
      5 tablespoons butter, melted
      4 eggs
      2 egg yolks
      3 cups milk
      1 cup heavy whipping cream
  1/2 cup sugar
      1 tablespoon vanilla extract
  1/4 teaspoon ground nutmeg
Confectioners' sugar, optional

Brush both sides of bread with butter; place in a greased 13-in. x 9-in. x 2-in. baking dish. In a large bowl, beat eggs and yolks. Add milk, cream, sugar, vanilla and nutmeg; mix well. Pour over the bread slices. Cover and chill overnight. Remove from the refrigerator 30 minutes before baking.

Bake, uncovered, at 350° for 55-60 minutes or until a knife inserted near the center comes out clean. Cool 10 minutes before serving. Dust with confectioners' sugar if desired. **Yield:** 8-10 servings.

Sour Cream Peach Kuchen

Salsa Corn Cakes (p. 30)

Best of Country Breakfast & Brunch

Chapter 2

Dishes In Minutes

When time's short in the morning, check this chapter. Every delicious dish can be prepared in just 30 minutes...or less!

Fruit Kabobs with Dip
Brunch Pizza Squares

Brunch Pizza Squares

LaChelle Olivet, Pace, Florida

I love cooking with convenience foods. When I serve these tasty squares made with refrigerated crescent rolls, guests always ask for the recipe.

☑ Uses less fat, sugar or salt. Includes Nutrition Facts and Diabetic Exchanges.

   1 **pound bulk pork sausage**
   1 **tube (8 ounces) refrigerated crescent rolls**
   4 **eggs**
   2 **tablespoons milk**
1/8 **teaspoon pepper**
3/4 **cup shredded cheddar cheese**

In a skillet, cook sausage over medium heat until no longer pink; drain. Unroll crescent dough into a lightly greased 13-in. x 9-in. x 2-in. baking pan. Press dough 1/2 in. up the sides; seal seams. Sprinkle with sausage. In a bowl, beat the eggs, milk and pepper; pour over sausage. Sprinkle with cheese.

Bake, uncovered, at 400° for 15 minutes or until the crust is golden brown and the cheese is melted. **Yield:** 8 servings.

Nutrition Facts: One serving (prepared with turkey sausage, egg substitute equivalent to 4 eggs, fat-free milk and reduced-fat crescent rolls and cheese) equals 243 calories, 13 g fat (0 saturated fat), 50 mg cholesterol, 687 mg sodium, 14 g carbohydrate, 1 g fiber, 18 g protein. **Diabetic Exchanges:** 2 meat, 1 starch, 1/2 fat.

Fruit Kabobs with Dip

LaChelle Olivet, Pace, Florida

Sweetened with honey, the banana-flavored dip for these kabobs is easy to make. It's a fun way to eat fresh fruit.

Assorted fruit—green grapes, watermelon balls, cantaloupe balls and strawberry halves
   1 **cup (8 ounces) plain yogurt**
1/2 **medium ripe banana**
   4 **teaspoons honey**
1/8 **teaspoon ground cinnamon**

Thread grapes, melon and berries alternately onto skewers. In a blender, combine remaining ingredients; cover and process until smooth. Serve with kabobs. **Yield:** 1-1/2 cups dip.

Strawberry Spread

Ruth Hodges, Harrisonville, Missouri

A friend gave me the simple recipe for this yummy spread years ago, and I've been enjoying it on many kinds of breads ever since.

   1 **package (8 ounces) cream cheese, softened**
   2 **tablespoons confectioners' sugar**
   3 **fresh strawberries, mashed**

In a mixing bowl, beat cream cheese and confectioners' sugar until smooth. Add strawberries; mix well. Serve on bagels, English muffins or toast. **Yield:** about 1 cup.

Tart Grapefruit Cooler

Connie Cooper, Charleston, Illinois

I pour this pretty pink beverage over ice to make a refreshing breakfast drink. The tart grapefruit juice always wakes up your taste buds.

☑ **Uses less fat, sugar or salt. Includes Nutrition Facts and Diabetic Exchanges.**

1-1/2 cups cranberry juice
    1 cup grapefruit juice
 1/2 cup sugar
 1/4 cup lemon juice
    1 cup club soda, chilled

In a bowl or pitcher, combine cranberry juice, grapefruit juice, sugar and lemon juice. Cover and refrigerate. Just before serving, stir in soda. **Yield:** 4 servings.

Nutrition Facts: One serving (prepared with unsweetened cranberry and grapefruit juices and artificial sweetener equivalent to 1/2 cup sugar) equals 57 calories, 16 mg sodium, 0 cholesterol, 14 g carbohydrate, trace protein, trace fat, trace fiber. **Diabetic Exchange:** 1 fruit.

Quick Cherry Turnovers

Elleen Oberrueter, Danbury, Iowa

These fruit-filled pastries are my family's favorite for breakfast. They're just as scrumptious with blueberry or apple pie filling instead of cherry.

1 tube (8 ounces) refrigerated crescent rolls
1 cup cherry pie filling

Quick Cherry Turnovers

Pepperoni Frittata

1/2 cup confectioners' sugar
   1 to 2 tablespoons milk

Unroll dough and separate into eight triangles; make four squares by pressing the seams of two triangles together and rolling into shape. Place on an ungreased baking sheet.

Spoon 1/4 cup filling in one corner of each square. Fold to make triangles; pinch to seal. Bake at 375° for 10-12 minutes or until golden. Mix sugar and milk; drizzle over turnovers. Serve warm. **Yield:** 4 servings.

Pepperoni Frittata

Nancy Daly, Douglas, Wyoming

We enjoy this delicious egg dish with fresh fruit and toast. It's a meal that makes a great weeknight supper, too.

1-1/4 cups chopped onions
   2 to 3 tablespoons vegetable oil
    1 cup sliced zucchini
 1/2 cup small cauliflowerets
    5 eggs, beaten
   26 slices pepperoni
 1/3 cup grated Parmesan cheese

In a 10-in. ovenproof skillet, saute the onions in oil until tender. Add the zucchini, cauliflower and eggs. Cover and cook over medium heat for 10-15 minutes or until eggs are nearly set.

Arrange pepperoni over eggs. Broil 6 in. from the heat for 2 minutes. Sprinkle with Parmesan cheese; broil 1-2 minutes longer or until eggs are completely set and top is lightly browned. Cut into wedges. **Yield:** 6 servings.

Chocolate Croissants

4 eggs
1 cup milk
Dash salt
1 can (21 ounces) apple *or* peach pie filling
Toasted walnuts, optional

Place butter in a 10-in. ovenproof skillet. Place in a 425° oven until melted. In a large mixing bowl, beat the flour, eggs, milk and salt until smooth. Leaving 1 tablespoon melted butter in the skillet, pour the remaining butter into the batter; mix until blended. Pour batter into hot skillet. Bake for 15-20 minutes or until edges are golden brown.

In a small saucepan, warm pie filling over low heat until heated through. Pour into center of puff pancake. Sprinkle with walnuts if desired. Serve immediately. **Yield:** 4 servings.

Chocolate Croissants

Phyllis Johnston, Fayetteville, Tennessee

Every now and then, we have stuffed French toast made from rich, buttery brioche. One Father's Day when I wanted to make it for my husband, the store was out of brioche, so I tried croissants instead. They turned out to be even simpler to use…and just as delicious!

   12 unsliced croissants
    2 cups milk chocolate chips
  1/3 cup sugar
    1 teaspoon cornstarch
    1 teaspoon ground cinnamon
    1 cup milk
    4 eggs, lightly beaten
  1/2 cup half-and-half cream
    3 teaspoons vanilla extract

Cut a slit into the side of each croissant; fill with about 2 tablespoons chocolate chips. In a shallow bowl, combine the sugar, cornstarch and cinnamon; whisk in the milk until smooth. Whisk in the eggs, half-and-half cream and vanilla.

Dip the croissants into egg mixture. Place in two greased 15-in. x 10-in. x 1-in. baking pans. Bake at 400° for 7-9 minutes or until golden brown. Serve warm. **Yield:** 1 dozen.

Apple Puff Pancake

Linda Hubbuch, Versailles, Kentucky

This thick and puffy pancake gets high praise from family and company alike. For an extra-special touch, top each serving with warm pancake syrup and whipped cream. You could also replace the apple pie filling with peach.

  1/3 cup butter
    1 cup all-purpose flour

Sweet Pineapple Muffins

Tina Hanson, Portage, Wisconsin

The refreshing flavor of pineapple really shines through in these yummy muffins. They're guaranteed to be gobbled up in no time!

    2 cups all-purpose flour
    2 cups sugar
    1 teaspoon baking soda
    1 teaspoon baking powder
    2 cans (8 ounces *each*) crushed pineapple, undrained
    2 eggs
  1/2 cup vegetable oil

In a large bowl, combine the flour, sugar, baking soda and baking powder. In another bowl, mix the undrained

Apple Puff Pancake

pineapple, eggs and oil; stir into the dry ingredients just until moistened.

Fill greased or paper-lined muffin cups two-thirds full. Bake at 350° for 20-25 minutes or until a toothpick comes out clean. Cool in pan for 10 minutes before removing to a wire rack. **Yield:** about 20 muffins.

Peach Waffle Syrup

Kristina Dalton, Coker, Alabama

I like to make this sweet, chunky syrup on leisurely weekend mornings as a special topping for waffles. Feel free to substitute fresh or canned peaches for the frozen ones called for in the recipe.

☑ **Uses less fat, sugar or salt. Includes Nutrition Facts and Diabetic Exchanges.**

- 1 package (20 ounces) frozen unsweetened peach slices, thawed and chopped
- 2 cups water
- 1/2 to 2/3 cup confectioners' sugar
- 1/8 teaspoon ground cinnamon
- 1 tablespoon cornstarch
- 2 tablespoons cold water

In a large saucepan, combine the peaches, water, confectioners' sugar and cinnamon. Bring to a boil. Reduce heat; simmer, uncovered, for 20 minutes.

Combine the cornstarch and cold water until smooth; gradually add to the peach mixture. Bring to a boil; cook and stir for 2 minutes or until thickened. **Yield:** about 3-1/2 cups.

Nutrition Facts: One 1/4-cup serving (prepared with 1/2 cup confectioners' sugar) equals 54 calories, trace fat (trace saturated fat), 0 cholesterol, 3 mg sodium, 14 g carbohydrate, 1 g fiber, trace protein. **Diabetic Exchange:** 1 fruit.

Cappuccino Smoothies

Michelle Cluney, Lake Mary, Florida

Topped with miniature marshmallows, this icy cappuccino beverage is a tempting twist on traditional fruit smoothies. My mom and I came up with it when we were trying to create a quick and easy treat.

- 1 cup (8 ounces) cappuccino *or* coffee yogurt
- 1/3 cup milk
- 3 tablespoons confectioners' sugar, optional
- 1 tablespoon chocolate syrup
- 1-1/2 cups ice cubes
- 1/2 cup miniature marshmallows, *divided*

In a blender, combine the yogurt, milk, confectioners' sugar if desired and chocolate syrup. Add the ice cubes and 1/4 cup marshmallows; cover and process until blended. Pour into chilled glasses; top smoothies with

French Toast Sticks

the remaining marshmallows. Serve immediately. **Yield:** 3 servings.

French Toast Sticks

Perfect for busy mornings, these strips of French toast from our Test Kitchen staff are stored in the freezer so you can pop them in the oven any time you like.

- 6 slices day-old Texas toast
- 4 eggs
- 1 cup milk
- 2 tablespoons sugar
- 1 teaspoon vanilla extract
- 1/4 to 1/2 teaspoon ground cinnamon
- 1 cup crushed cornflakes, optional

Confectioners' sugar, optional
Maple syrup

Cut each piece of bread into thirds; place in an ungreased 13-in. x 9-in. x 2-in. dish. In a large bowl, whisk the eggs, milk, sugar, vanilla and cinnamon. Pour over the bread pieces; soak for 2 minutes, turning them over once.

If desired, coat bread with cornflake crumbs on all sides. Place in a greased 15-in. x 10-in. x 1-in. baking pan. Freeze until firm, about 45 minutes. Transfer to an airtight container or resealable freezer bag and store in the freezer.

To bake, place desired number of frozen French toast sticks on a greased baking sheet. Bake at 425° for 8 minutes. Turn; bake 10-12 minutes longer or until golden brown. Sprinkle with confectioners' sugar if desired. Serve with syrup. **Yield:** 1-1/2 dozen.

Very Veggie Omelet

Very Veggie Omelet

Jan Houberg, Reddick, Illinois

I surprised my husband, who loves to sample new dishes, with this light and fluffy omelet full of garden goodness.

✓ **Uses less fat, sugar or salt. Includes Nutrition Facts and Diabetic Exchanges.**

- 1 **small onion, chopped**
- 1/4 **cup chopped green pepper**
- 1 **tablespoon butter**
- 1 **small zucchini, chopped**
- 3/4 **cup chopped tomato**
- 1/4 **teaspoon dried oregano**
- 1/8 **teaspoon pepper**
- 4 **egg whites**
- 1/4 **cup water**
- 1/4 **teaspoon cream of tartar**
- 1/4 **teaspoon salt**
- 1/4 **cup egg substitute**
- 1/2 **cup shredded reduced-fat cheddar cheese, divided**

In a large nonstick skillet, saute onion and green pepper in butter until tender. Add the zucchini, tomato, oregano and pepper. Cook and stir for 5-8 minutes or until vegetables are tender and liquid is nearly evaporated. Set aside and keep warm. In a mixing bowl, beat egg whites, water, cream of tartar and salt until stiff peaks form. Place egg substitute in another bowl; fold in egg white mixture.

Pour into a 10-in. ovenproof skillet coated with nonstick cooking spray. Cook over medium heat for 5 minutes or until bottom is lightly browned. Bake at 350°

for 9-10 minutes or until a knife inserted near the center comes out clean. Spoon vegetable mixture over one side; sprinkle with half of the cheese. To fold, score middle of omelet with a sharp knife; fold omelet over filling. Transfer to a warm platter. Sprinkle with remaining cheese. Cut in half to serve. **Yield:** 2 servings.

Nutrition Facts: One serving (half an omelet) equals 197 calories, 9 g fat (5 g saturated fat), 21 mg cholesterol, 639 mg sodium, 10 g carbohydrate, 2 g fiber, 19 g protein. **Diabetic Exchanges:** 2-1/2 lean meat, 2 vegetable.

Cinnamon Biscuits

These nicely spiced biscuits from the Taste of Home Test Kitchen will disappear as quickly as you can serve them! Try them for breakfast, as a snack or even with fried chicken.

- 2 **cups all-purpose flour**
- 1 **tablespoon baking powder**
- 2 **teaspoons sugar**
- 1/2 **teaspoon salt**
- 1/4 **teaspoon ground cinnamon**
- 1/4 **cup cold butter**
- 1 **cup milk**

Melted butter
Cinnamon-sugar

In a bowl, combine dry ingredients; cut in butter until crumbly. Stir in milk just until moistened. Drop by 1/4 cupfuls onto a greased baking sheet. Brush with melted butter and sprinkle with cinnamon-sugar. Bake at 450° for 10-12 minutes or until lightly browned. Serve warm. **Yield:** about 1 dozen.

Apricot Cream-Filled Waffles

Dorothy Smith, El Dorado, Arkansas

These scrumptious waffles are perfect for Christmas morning because they won't keep you in the kitchen long. The rich, creamy filling can be whipped up in a snap.

- 1 package (3 ounces) cream cheese, softened
- 1 to 2 tablespoons honey
- 2/3 cup chopped canned apricots
- 8 frozen waffles, toasted
- 1/2 cup maple syrup, warmed

In a small bowl, combine cream cheese and honey; mix well. Stir in apricots. Spread cream cheese mixture on four waffles; top with remaining waffles. Serve with syrup. **Yield:** 4 servings.

Cherry Berry Smoothies

Macy Plummer, Avon, Indiana

You need just four ingredients to blend together these super-fast smoothies for breakfast. They're also great as a cool treat on a hot summer afternoon.

- 1-1/2 cups unsweetened apple juice
- 1 cup frozen unsweetened raspberries
- 1 cup frozen pitted dark sweet cherries
- 1-1/2 cups raspberry sherbet

In a blender, combine the apple juice, raspberries and cherries. Add sherbet; cover and process until well blended. Pour into chilled glasses; serve immediately. **Yield:** 4 servings.

Cherry Berry Smoothies

Cinnamon Rolls in a Snap

Cinnamon Rolls in a Snap

Laura McDermott, Big Lake, Minnesota

I turned biscuits into hot cinnamon rolls one morning because a friend was stopping by. She was so impressed, I felt like a gourmet cook!

- 4-1/2 cups biscuit/baking mix
- 1-1/3 cups milk
- FILLING:
    - 2 tablespoons butter, softened
    - 1/4 cup sugar
    - 1 teaspoon ground cinnamon
    - 1/3 cup raisins, optional
- ICING:
    - 2 cups confectioners' sugar
    - 2 tablespoons milk
    - 2 tablespoons butter, melted
    - 1 teaspoon vanilla extract

In a bowl, combine biscuit mix and milk. Turn onto a floured surface; knead 8-10 times. Roll the dough into a 12-in. x 10-in. rectangle. Spread with butter. Combine sugar, cinnamon and raisins if desired; sprinkle over the butter.

Roll up from a long side; pinch seam to seal. Cut into 12 slices; place with cut side down on a large greased baking sheet. Bake at 450° for 10-12 minutes or until golden brown. Meanwhile, combine the icing ingredients; spread over rolls. Serve warm. **Yield:** 1 dozen.

Cherry Almond Granola

Cherry Almond Granola

Deborah Purdue, Freeland, Michigan

Skim milk turns this crunchy snack into a healthy breakfast cereal, while a dollop of low-fat yogurt makes it a yummy dessert. Try adding a little baking cocoa to the brown sugar for a taste twist.

☑ **Uses less fat, sugar or salt. Includes Nutrition Facts and Diabetic Exchanges.**

- 1 cup packed brown sugar
- 1/2 cup nonfat dry milk powder
- 1/2 cup honey
- 1/3 cup unsweetened apple juice concentrate
- 2 tablespoons canola oil
- 3 teaspoons almond extract
- 6 cups old-fashioned oats
- 1-1/2 cups dried cherries *or* cranberries
- 1 cup slivered almonds

Fat-free vanilla yogurt, optional

In a saucepan, combine the brown sugar, dry milk powder, honey, apple juice concentrate and oil. Cook and stir over medium heat until the sugar is dissolved; stir in almond extract. In a large bowl, combine the oats, dried cherries and almonds. Drizzle with the sugar mixture and mix well.

Spread in a thin layer in two 15-in. x 10-in. x 1-in. baking pans coated with nonstick cooking spray. Bake at

375° for 15-20 minutes or until golden brown, stirring occasionally. Cool completely. Serve with yogurt if desired. Store in an airtight container. **Yield:** 3 quarts.

Nutrition Facts: One serving (1/2 cup granola) equals 222 calories, 5 g fat (1 g saturated fat), trace cholesterol, 15 mg sodium, 38 g carbohydrate, 3 g fiber, 5 g protein. **Diabetic Exchanges:** 1-1/2 fruit, 1 starch, 1 fat.

Asparagus Eggs Benedict

Mark Morgan, Waterford, Wisconsin

This is a favorite Sunday brunch dish at our house during spring. If I'm not pressed for time, I'll make a hollandaise sauce from scratch.

- 12 fresh asparagus spears, trimmed and cut in half
- 1 envelope hollandaise sauce mix
- 6 eggs
- 3 English muffins, split and toasted
- 1/2 cup shredded Swiss cheese

Paprika

Place the asparagus spears in a steamer basket. Place in a large saucepan over 1 in. of water; bring to a boil. Cover and steam for 3-4 minutes or until crisp-tender. Set aside.

Prepare hollandaise sauce according to package directions. Meanwhile, in a large skillet, bring 2-3 in. water to a boil. Reduce heat; simmer gently. Break cold eggs, one at a time, into a custard cup or saucer. Holding the dish close to the surface of the water, slip the eggs, one at a time, into the water. Cook, uncovered, for 3-5 minutes or until the whites are completely set and the yolks begin to thicken. With a slotted

Asparagus Eggs Benedict

spoon, lift each egg out of the water.

To assemble, place 4 pieces of asparagus on each muffin half; top with a poached egg, then sprinkle with cheese. Top each with about 3 tablespoons hollandaise sauce; garnish with paprika. Serve immediately. **Yield:** 6 servings.

Fruity French Toast

Nancy Hawthorne, Gettysburg, Pennsylvania

My son begged me to try making the fruit-stuffed French toast we enjoyed during our trip to Walt Disney World. The easy variation I came up with is now a weekend favorite.

  1 **medium firm banana, sliced**
  4 **slices Texas toast**
  2 **teaspoons confectioners' sugar,** *divided*
  2 **large strawberries, sliced**
  1 **egg**
1/2 **cup milk**
1/2 **teaspoon vanilla extract**
1/4 **teaspoon ground cinnamon**
  2 **teaspoons butter**
Maple syrup

Place banana slices on two slices of toast. Sprinkle each with 1/2 teaspoon confectioners' sugar. Top with strawberries and remaining toast. In a shallow bowl, whisk the egg, milk, vanilla and cinnamon. Dip toast in egg mixture, coating both sides.

In a large skillet, melt butter over medium heat; cook toast for 2-4 minutes on each side or until golden brown. Sprinkle with remaining confectioners' sugar. Serve with maple syrup. **Yield:** 2 servings.

Banana-Toffee Muffin Tops

Betty Kleberger, Florissant, Missouri

Toffee bits and bananas give these moist breakfast treats fantastic flavor. For an extra-special look, top them with a sprinkling of coarse sugar crystals.

2-1/2 **cups biscuit/baking mix**
 1/3 **cup English toffee bits** *or* **almond brickle chips**
 1/4 **cup sugar**
   1 **egg**
 1/4 **cup heavy whipping cream**
 1/2 **teaspoon vanilla extract**
   1 **cup mashed ripe bananas (about 2 medium)**
Additional sugar

In a bowl, combine biscuit mix, toffee and sugar. In another bowl, combine egg, cream and vanilla; stir in bananas. Stir into dry ingredients just until combined.

Drop by tablespoonfuls onto greased baking sheets.

Fruity French Toast

Sprinkle with additional sugar. Bake at 425° for 11-13 minutes or until golden brown. Remove to wire racks. Serve warm. **Yield:** about 1-1/2 dozen.

Sunny Citrus Cooler

Holly Joyce, Jackson, Minnesota

People often request a second glass of this tangy blend of fruit juices, lemonade and ginger ale. The good news is, it's easy to stir up another gallon if you need to!

  1 **can (46 ounces) pineapple juice**
  2 **cans (12 ounces** *each***) frozen orange juice concentrate, thawed**
3/4 **cup lemonade concentrate**
  6 **cups ginger ale** *or* **white soda, chilled**
Orange slices, optional

In a 1-gal. pitcher, combine pineapple juice, orange juice concentrate and lemonade concentrate. Add ginger ale and mix well. Serve over ice. Garnish with orange slices if desired. Refrigerate leftovers. **Yield:** 1 gallon.

Flavor Savers

Consider making extra Sunny Citrus Cooler (on this page) and using it instead of water to make ice cubes. Your beverage won't get a watered-down taste as the ice melts.

Sunrise Orange Pancakes

Sunrise Orange Pancakes

Dorothy Smith, El Dorado, Arkansas

These delectable, citrusy pancakes make any breakfast seem special. Plus, they're simple enough to prepare on a busy weekday morning.

    7 tablespoons sugar, *divided*
1-1/2 teaspoons cornstarch
1-1/2 cups orange juice, *divided*
    2 cups biscuit/baking mix
    2 eggs
  3/4 cup milk

In a saucepan, combine 4 tablespoons sugar, cornstarch and 3/4 cup orange juice; stir until smooth. Bring to a boil; cook and stir for 2 minutes. Remove from heat; cool to lukewarm.

Meanwhile, combine biscuit mix and remaining sugar in a bowl. Beat the eggs, milk and remaining orange juice; stir into dry ingredients just until moistened. Pour the batter by 1/4 cupfuls onto a lightly greased hot griddle; turn when bubbles form on top of pancakes. Cook until second side is golden brown. Serve with the orange sauce. **Yield:** 1 dozen.

Salsa Corn Cakes

(Pictured on page 20)

Lisa Boettcher, Rosebush, Michigan

This recipe is super with either fresh or canned corn. I sometimes pair these cakes with nachos or tacos for dinner.

1-1/2 cups all-purpose flour
  1/2 cup cornmeal
    1 teaspoon baking powder
    1 teaspoon salt

    2 packages (3 ounces *each*) cream cheese, softened
    6 eggs
    1 cup milk
  1/4 cup butter, melted
    1 can (15-1/4 ounces) whole kernel corn, drained
  1/2 cup salsa, drained
  1/4 cup minced green onions
Sour cream and additional salsa

Combine flour, cornmeal, baking powder and salt; set aside. In a mixing bowl, beat cream cheese and eggs; add milk and butter. Add the dry ingredients just until moistened. Fold in the corn, salsa and onions.

Pour batter by 1/4 cupfuls onto a greased hot griddle. Turn when bubbles form on top; cook until the second side is golden brown. Serve with sour cream and salsa. **Yield:** 6-8 servings.

Coconut Toast

Betty Checkett, St. Louis, Missouri

The sweet and buttery coconut topping on this toasty bread is absolutely scrumptious. Enjoy slices with a cup of coffee at breakfast or for a snack any time of day.

    1 cup flaked coconut
    1 cup sugar
  1/2 cup butter, melted
    1 egg, beaten
    1 teaspoon vanilla extract
  11 to 12 slices white bread

In a bowl, combine coconut, sugar, butter, egg and vanilla; mix well. Spread over each slice of bread; place on ungreased baking sheets. Bake at 350° for 15-20 minutes or until lightly browned. **Yield:** 11-12 servings.

Coconut Toast

Sausage Potato Skillet

Sausage Potato Skillet

Here, our Test Kitchen home economists combined two popular breakfast side dishes—sausage links and hash brown potatoes—which are conveniently cooked in the same skillet.

- 1 package (8 ounces) brown-and-serve sausage links
- 2 tablespoons water
- 2 tablespoons vegetable oil
- 3 cups frozen shredded hash brown potatoes
- 1/2 cup chopped sweet red *or* green pepper
- 1/4 cup chopped onion

Salt and pepper to taste

Cut sausage links into bite-size pieces. In a covered skillet, cook sausage in water and oil over medium heat for 5 minutes. Remove sausage with a slotted spoon and keep warm.

Carefully add potatoes, red pepper and onion to pan. Cover and cook for 5 minutes. Uncover; cook 5-6 minutes longer or until potatoes are tender. Return sausage to pan; heat through. Season with salt and pepper. **Yield:** 4 servings.

Zippy Praline Bacon

Myrt Pfannkuche, Pell City, Alabama

Just three simple ingredients give this bacon an entirely new and delicious taste. You'll want to make it regularly.

- 1 pound sliced bacon
- 3 tablespoons brown sugar
- 1-1/2 teaspoons chili powder
- 1/4 cup finely chopped pecans

Line two 15-in. x 10-in. x 1-in. baking pans with foil. Arrange bacon in a single layer in pans. Bake at 425° for 10 minutes; drain.

Combine the brown sugar and chili powder; sprinkle over bacon. Sprinkle with pecans. Bake 5-10 minutes longer or until bacon is crisp. Drain on paper towels. **Yield:** 10 servings.

Peach Smoothies

Dana Tittle, Forest City, Alaska

To me, there's no sweeter start to the day than this mellow, refreshing beverage. It's great as a pick-me-up in the afternoon, too. Using frozen sliced peaches means you don't have to cut any fruit.

- 2 cups milk
- 2 cups frozen unsweetened sliced peaches
- 1/4 cup orange juice concentrate
- 2 tablespoons sugar
- 5 ice cubes

In a blender, combine all ingredients; cover and process until smooth. Pour into glasses; serve immediately. **Yield:** 4 servings.

Fiesta Scrambled Eggs

Fiesta Scrambled Eggs

Kay Kropff, Canyon, Texas

I love to fix this spicy scrambled egg dish for friends and family. It's a meal in itself, but I serve it with muffins or biscuits, fresh fruit juice and coffee.

      1/2 cup chopped onion
      1/4 cup chopped sweet red pepper
        1 jalapeno pepper, seeded and chopped
        8 bacon strips, cooked and crumbled
        8 eggs, lightly beaten
        1 cup (4 ounces) shredded cheddar cheese, *divided*
      1/2 teaspoon salt
      1/8 teaspoon pepper
Salsa

In a large nonstick skillet coated with nonstick cooking spray, saute the onion and peppers until tender. Sprinkle with bacon. Pour eggs over the top; sprinkle with 1/2 cup cheese, salt and pepper. Cook over medium heat, stirring occasionally, until eggs are completely set. Sprinkle with remaining cheese. Serve with salsa. **Yield:** 6 servings.

   Editor's Note: When cutting or seeding hot peppers, use rubber or plastic gloves to protect your hands. Avoid touching your face.

Strawberry Granola Squares

Most of the ingredients in these yummy squares, created in the Taste of Home Test Kitchen, can be found in your pantry. Plus, you can freeze any extras to enjoy later on.

  1-1/2 cups granola cereal without raisins
      3/4 cup all-purpose flour
      1/3 cup packed brown sugar
      1/2 teaspoon ground cinnamon
        5 tablespoons cold butter
        1 cup strawberry preserves

In a large bowl, combine the granola, flour, brown sugar and cinnamon; cut in butter until crumbly. Set aside a third of the mixture for topping. Press remaining mixture into a well-greased 9-in. square baking pan. Bake at 375° for 10 minutes.

   Spread strawberry preserves over crust; sprinkle with the reserved granola mixture. Bake 15 minutes longer or until filling is bubbly around the edges. Cool on a wire rack. Cut into squares. Store in the refrigerator. **Yield:** 16 squares.

Camper's Breakfast Hash

Linda Krivanek, Oak Creek, Wisconsin

When we go camping with family and friends, I'm always asked to make this cheesy sausage, egg and potato breakfast. It's so easy—everything cooks in the same skillet. Everyone's ready for a big day of outdoor activities after enjoying this hearty, meal-in-one hash.

      1/4 cup butter, cubed
        2 packages (20 ounces *each*) refrigerated shredded hash brown potatoes
        1 package (7 ounces) brown-and-serve sausage links, cut into 1/2-inch pieces
      1/4 cup chopped onion
      1/4 cup chopped green pepper
       12 eggs, lightly beaten

Camper's Breakfast Hash

Salt and pepper to taste
   1 cup (4 ounces) shredded cheddar cheese

In a large skillet, melt butter. Add the potatoes, sausage, onion and green pepper. Cook, uncovered, over medium heat for 10-15 minutes or until potatoes are lightly browned, turning once.

Push potato mixture to the sides of pan. Pour eggs into center of pan. Cook and stir over medium heat until eggs are completely set. Season with salt and pepper. Reduce heat; stir eggs into potato mixture. Top with cheese; cover and cook for 1-2 minutes or until cheese is melted. **Yield:** 8 servings.

Sausage Gravy with Biscuits

Alyce Wyman, Pembina, North Dakota

This down-home dish is terrific for breakfast, but my husband and I also enjoy it with a tossed salad for dinner.

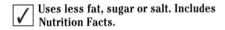

✓ **Uses less fat, sugar or salt. Includes Nutrition Facts.**

   2 individually frozen biscuits
   1/4 pound bulk pork sausage
   3 tablespoons all-purpose flour
   1/4 teaspoon salt, optional
   1/4 teaspoon Italian seasoning
   1/4 teaspoon rubbed sage
   1/8 teaspoon garlic powder
   1/8 teaspoon pepper
 1-1/2 cups 2% milk

Bake biscuits according to package directions. Meanwhile, crumble sausage into a small skillet. Cook over medium heat until no longer pink; drain. Stir in flour and seasonings until blended. Gradually add milk. Bring to a boil; cook and stir for 2 minutes or until thickened. Split biscuits in half; serve with sausage gravy. **Yield:** 2 servings.

Nutrition Facts: 1 biscuit with 3/4 cup sausage gravy (prepared with reduced-fat sausage and fat-free milk) equals 444 calories, 22 g fat (7 g saturated fat), 44 mg cholesterol, 1,105 mg sodium, 42 g carbohydrate, 1 g fiber, 21 g protein.

Fruit Medley

Becky Hughes, Las Cruces, New Mexico

This is a variation of a fruit salad from my husband's aunt. The original recipe calls for a homemade glaze, but I use canned peach pie filling to hurry along preparation.

   1 can (21 ounces) peach pie filling
   1 can (20 ounces) pineapple chunks, drained
   1 can (11 ounces) mandarin oranges, drained
   1 jar (10 ounces) maraschino cherries, drained

Iced Coffee

   2 medium firm bananas, sliced
   1/2 cup chopped pecans

In a bowl, combine the pie filling, pineapple, oranges, cherries and bananas. Cover and refrigerate. Just before serving, stir in pecans. **Yield:** 8-10 servings.

Iced Coffee

Jenny Reece, Lowry, Minnesota

When I first discovered iced coffee, I wasn't sure I'd like it. Then I created this fast-to-fix version and found it to be a refreshing alternative to hot coffee. Using sugar substitute and fat-free milk makes this recipe nice for people who are watching their diet.

✓ **Uses less fat, sugar or salt. Includes Nutrition Facts and Diabetic Exchanges.**

   4 teaspoons instant coffee granules
   1 cup boiling water
Sugar substitute equivalent to 4 teaspoons sugar, optional
   1 cup fat-free milk
   4 teaspoons chocolate syrup
   1/8 teaspoon vanilla extract
Ice cubes

In a large bowl, dissolve coffee in water. Add sweetener if desired. Stir in the milk, chocolate syrup and vanilla; mix well. Serve over ice. **Yield:** 2 cups.

Nutrition Facts: 1 cup equals 79 calories, 1 g fat (0 saturated fat), 2 mg cholesterol, 76 mg sodium, 15 g carbohydrate, 0 fiber, 5 g protein. **Diabetic Exchanges:** 1/2 starch, 1/2 fat-free milk.

Editor's Note: This recipe was tested with Splenda No Calorie Sweetener.

Frozen Banana Pineapple Cups (p. 40)

Best of Country Breakfast & Brunch

Chapter 3

Overnight Delights

Pop these make-ahead favorites in the fridge or freezer the night before…and enjoy a scrumptious breakfast in a snap!

Spinach Cheese Phyllo Squares

Spinach Cheese Phyllo Squares

Julie Remer, Gahanna, Ohio

A higher-fat version of this layered bake was always a hit when my aunt and I ran a gourmet carryout business. Now that I'm cooking only for my family, I lightened up this dish a bit, and everyone still enjoys it.

✓ **Uses less fat, sugar or salt. Includes Nutrition Facts and Diabetic Exchanges.**

  6 sheets phyllo dough (14 inches x 9 inches)
  1 package (10 ounces) frozen chopped spinach, thawed and squeezed dry
2-1/2 cups (10 ounces) shredded part-skim mozzarella cheese
1-1/2 cups (6 ounces) shredded reduced-fat cheddar cheese
1-1/2 cups fat-free cottage cheese
  4 eggs
1-1/2 teaspoons dried parsley flakes
 3/4 teaspoon salt
  6 egg whites
1-1/2 cups fat-free milk

Layer three sheets of phyllo dough in a 13-in. x 9-in. x 2-in. baking dish coated with nonstick cooking spray, lightly spraying the top of each sheet with nonstick cooking spray.

In a bowl, combine the spinach, cheese, 2 eggs, parsley flakes and salt; spread over phyllo dough. Top with remaining phyllo sheets, lightly spraying the top of each sheet with nonstick cooking spray. Using a sharp knife, cut into 12 squares; cover and chill for 1 hour.

Beat egg whites, milk and remaining eggs; pour over casserole. Cover and refrigerate overnight.

Remove from the refrigerator 1 hour before baking. Bake, uncovered, at 375° for 40-50 minutes or until a knife inserted near the center comes out clean and top is golden brown. Let stand for 10 minutes before cutting. **Yield:** 12 servings.

Nutrition Facts: 1 piece equals 187 calories, 9 g fat (5 g saturated fat), 97 mg cholesterol, 593 mg sodium, 9 g carbohydrate, 1 g fiber, 19 g protein. **Diabetic Exchanges:** 2 lean meat, 1/2 starch, 1/2 fat.

Orange French Toast

Kristy Martin, Circle Pine, Minnesota

I use leftover slices of cinnamon bread to assemble this overnight brunch dish. With a hint of orange flavor, it's a special way to "wake up" weekend guests.

  6 eggs, lightly beaten
 3/4 cup orange juice
1/2 cup half-and-half cream
  2 tablespoons sugar
  1 teaspoon vanilla extract
1/2 teaspoon grated orange peel
  8 thick slices cinnamon bread
1/4 cup butter, melted

In a shallow bowl, combine the first six ingredients. Dip both sides of bread into egg mixture; let soak for 5 minutes. Place in a greased 15-in. x 10-in. x 1-in. baking pan. Cover and refrigerate overnight.

Uncover; drizzle with butter. Bake at 325° for 35-40 minutes or until browned. **Yield:** 8 servings.

Orange French Toast

Farmer's Casserole

Nancy Schmidt, Center, Colorado

The flavors blend wonderfully as this delicious casserole sits in the refrigerator overnight. It's also versatile—elegant enough to serve for a ladies' brunch but hearty enough to satisfy a man-sized appetite.

- 3 cups frozen shredded hash brown potatoes
- 3/4 cup shredded Monterey Jack cheese
- 1 cup diced fully cooked ham
- 1/4 cup chopped green onions
- 4 eggs
- 1 can (12 ounces) evaporated milk
- 1/4 teaspoon pepper
- 1/8 teaspoon salt

Place potatoes in an 8-in. square baking dish. Sprinkle with cheese, ham and onions. Beat eggs, milk, pepper and salt; pour over all. Cover and refrigerate for several hours or overnight.

Remove from refrigerator 30 minutes before baking. Bake, uncovered, at 350° for 55-60 minutes or until a knife inserted near the center comes out clean. Let stand for 10 minutes before serving. **Yield:** 6 servings.

Chili Cheese Strata

Shirley Smith, Anaheim, California

With plenty of cheese, salsa and green chilies, this make-ahead casserole has south-of-the-border flavor that pleases the whole family. If it suits your tastes, use a medium-hot or hot variety of salsa.

- 1 loaf (12 ounces) French bread, cut into 1-inch cubes
- 2 cups shredded cheddar *or* Monterey Jack cheese, *divided*
- 1 jar (8 ounces) mild green chili salsa *or* 4 ounces chopped green chilies and 4 ounces salsa, combined
- 4 eggs
- 1 can (10-3/4 ounces) condensed cheddar cheese soup, undiluted
- 2 cups milk *or* half-and-half cream
- 2 tablespoons finely chopped onion
- 1 teaspoon Worcestershire sauce

Place bread cubes evenly in a greased 2-qt. shallow baking dish. Sprinkle with 1 cup cheese. Pour salsa over cheese; set aside. In blender, combine eggs, soup, milk, onion and Worcestershire sauce; pour over bread mixture. Sprinkle with remaining cheese. Cover and refrigerate 6 hours or overnight.

Remove from the refrigerator 30 minutes before baking. Bake, uncovered, at 350° for 30 minutes or until a knife inserted near the center comes out clean. Let stand 10 minutes before serving. **Yield:** 8 servings.

Any-Season Fruit Bowl

Any-Season Fruit Bowl

Frances Stevenson, McRae, Georgia

A refreshing fruit salad like this one is always a welcome addition to morning meals. A hint of anise gives it a bit of holiday flavor...and it looks gorgeous on a buffet table, too.

- 2 cups water
- 1-1/2 cups sugar
- 1/3 cup lime *or* lemon juice
- 1 teaspoon anise extract
- 1/2 teaspoon salt
- 3 oranges, peeled and sectioned
- 3 kiwifruit, peeled and sliced
- 2 grapefruit, peeled and sectioned
- 2 large apples, cubed
- 1 pint strawberries, sliced
- 1 pound green grapes
- 1 can (20 ounces) pineapple chunks, drained

In a medium saucepan, combine water, sugar, lime juice, anise and salt. Bring to a boil over medium heat; cook for 20 minutes, stirring occasionally. Remove from the heat; cover and refrigerate for 6 hours or overnight.

Combine fruit in a large bowl; add dressing and toss to coat. Cover and chill for at least 1 hour. **Yield:** 16-18 servings.

Beyond Breakfast

Farmer's Casserole and Chili Cheese Strata (recipes on this page) are great choices for dinner, too. Assemble them in the morning, then bake them at suppertime.

Overnight Pancakes

Overnight Pancakes

Lisa Sammons, Cut Bank, Montana

These golden, fluffy pancakes are great for Sunday brunches with friends…and they get our kids off to a good start before school during the week. The buttermilk batter is refrigerated overnight to help ease the morning rush.

    1 **package (1/4 ounce) active dry yeast**
1/4 **cup warm water (110° to 115°)**
    4 **cups all-purpose flour**
    2 **tablespoons baking powder**
    2 **teaspoons baking soda**
    2 **teaspoons sugar**
    1 **teaspoon salt**
    6 **eggs**
    4 **cups buttermilk**
1/4 **cup vegetable oil**

In a small bowl, dissolve yeast in water; let stand for 5 minutes.

Meanwhile, in a large bowl, combine the dry ingredients. Beat eggs, buttermilk and oil; stir into dry ingredients just until moistened. Stir in yeast mixture. Cover and refrigerate for 8 hours or overnight.

To make pancakes, pour batter by 1/4 cupfuls onto a greased hot griddle; turn when bubbles form on top of pancakes. Cook until second side is golden brown. **Yield:** about 2-1/2 dozen.

Honey Bran Muffins

Pauline Rohloff, Endeavor, Wisconsin

When time is short and you want to serve fresh-from-the-oven muffins for breakfast or brunch, keep this make-ahead recipe in mind. You'll love it!

    2 **cups pineapple juice**
    2 **cups golden raisins**
    5 **eggs, beaten**
    1 **cup packed brown sugar**
1/2 **cup vegetable oil**
1/2 **cup honey**
    2 **cups all-purpose flour**
    2 **teaspoons baking soda**
    1 **teaspoon salt**
    4 **cups All-Bran**

In a small bowl, combine pineapple juice and raisins; set aside. In a large mixing bowl, combine brown sugar, oil, honey and eggs; mix well. Combine flour, baking soda and salt; stir in cereal. Add to sugar mixture and mix well. Fold in the raisin mixture (batter will be thin). Cover and refrigerate at least 3 hours or overnight.

Stir (batter will thicken). Fill greased or paper-lined muffin cups three-fourths full. Bake at 400° for 20-25 minutes or until a toothpick comes out clean. Cool in pan 10 minutes; remove to a wire rack. **Yield:** about 12 jumbo muffins or 20 standard-size muffins.

Italian Sausage Strata

Amanda Reid, Oakville, Iowa

This savory dish gives me extra time in the morning. All I have to do is pop the prepared casserole in the oven.

- 1/2 cup butter, softened, *divided*
- 12 to 16 slices day-old bread, crusts removed
- 1/2 pound fresh mushrooms, sliced
- 2 cups sliced onions

Salt and pepper to taste
- 1 pound bulk Italian sausage, cooked and drained
- 3 cups (12 ounces) shredded cheddar cheese
- 5 eggs
- 2-1/2 cups milk
- 1 tablespoon Dijon mustard
- 1 teaspoon ground nutmeg
- 1 teaspoon ground mustard
- 2 tablespoons minced fresh parsley

Using 1/4 cup butter, spread one side of each bread slice with butter. Place half of the bread, butter side down, in a greased 13-in. x 9-in. x 2-in. baking dish.

In a large skillet, saute the mushrooms and onions in remaining butter. Sprinkle with salt and pepper. Spoon half of the mushroom mixture over bread in prepared pan. Top with half of the sausage and cheese. Layer with the remaining bread, mushroom mixture, sausage and cheese. In a bowl, combine the eggs, milk, Dijon mustard, nutmeg and ground mustard. Pour over cheese. Cover and refrigerate overnight.

Remove from refrigerator 30 minutes before baking. Bake, covered, at 350° for 50 minutes. Uncover; bake 10-15 minutes longer or until a knife inserted near center comes out clean. Sprinkle with parsley. Let stand for 10 minutes before serving. **Yield:** 12 servings.

Coffee House Slush

Shannon Wade, Kansas City, Kansas

When you're making this special, coffee shop-like drink for breakfast, freeze it the day before and thaw it overnight so you'll have a slushy drink in the morning.

- 6 cups strong brewed coffee
- 2 cups sugar
- 2 quarts milk
- 1 quart half-and-half cream
- 4 teaspoons vanilla extract

Whipped cream

In a 5-qt. freezer container, stir coffee and sugar until sugar is dissolved. Stir in milk, cream and vanilla. Cover and freeze for 8 hours or overnight.

To serve, thaw in the refrigerator for 8-10 hours or until slushy. Spoon into glasses; garnish with whipped cream. **Yield:** 5 quarts.

Overnight Coffee Cake

Cindy Harris, San Antonio, Texas

Because this from-scratch cake is assembled the day before, it's a terrific time-saver. My kids think the nutty topping and sweet glaze make it the ultimate treat.

- 3/4 cup butter, softened
- 1 cup sugar
- 2 eggs
- 2 cups all-purpose flour
- 1 teaspoon baking soda
- 1 teaspoon ground nutmeg
- 1/2 teaspoon salt
- 1 cup (8 ounces) sour cream
- 3/4 cup packed brown sugar
- 1/2 cup chopped pecans *or* walnuts
- 1 teaspoon ground cinnamon
- 1-1/2 cups confectioners' sugar
- 3 tablespoons milk

In a large mixing bowl, cream butter and sugar. Add eggs, one at a time, beating well after each addition. Combine the flour, baking soda, nutmeg and salt; add to the creamed mixture alternately with sour cream. Pour into a greased 13-in. x 9-in. x 2-in. baking dish.

In a small bowl, combine the brown sugar, pecans and cinnamon; sprinkle over coffee cake. Cover and refrigerate overnight.

Remove from the refrigerator 30 minutes before baking. Bake, uncovered, at 350° for 35-40 minutes or until a toothpick inserted near the center comes out clean. Cool on a wire rack for 10 minutes. Combine confectioners' sugar and milk; drizzle over warm coffee cake. **Yield:** 12-15 servings.

Overnight Coffee Cake

Blueberry French Toast

Frozen Banana Pineapple Cups

(Pictured on page 34)

Alice Miller, Middlebury, Indiana

After you stir together this frosty medley, just pop it in the freezer for the next morning. In summer, our kids prefer this frozen treat over store-bought ones as a snack.

        3 cups water
    2-2/3 cups mashed ripe bananas (5 to 6 medium)
    1-1/2 cups sugar
        1 can (20 ounces) crushed pineapple,
          undrained
        1 can (6 ounces) frozen orange juice
          concentrate, thawed

In a 2-qt. freezer container, combine all ingredients; mix well. Cover and freeze for 5 hours or overnight. Remove from the freezer 15 minutes before serving. **Yield:** 9-12 servings.

Blueberry French Toast

Patricia Walls, Aurora, Minnesota

This is the best breakfast dish I've ever tasted! With blueberries inside and a luscious blueberry sauce, it almost seems like a dessert.

       12 slices day-old white bread, crusts removed
        2 packages (8 ounces *each*) cream cheese
        1 cup fresh *or* frozen blueberries
       12 eggs
        2 cups milk
      1/3 cup maple syrup *or* honey
SAUCE:
        1 cup sugar
        2 tablespoons cornstarch
        1 cup water
        1 cup fresh *or* frozen blueberries
        1 tablespoon butter

Cut bread into 1-in. cubes; place half in a greased 13-in. x 9-in. x 2-in. baking dish. Cut cream cheese into 1-in. cubes; place over bread. Top with blueberries and remaining bread cubes.

In a large bowl, beat eggs. Add milk and syrup; mix well. Pour over bread mixture. Cover and refrigerate for 8 hours or overnight.

Remove from the refrigerator 30 minutes before baking. Cover and bake at 350° for 30 minutes. Uncover; bake 25-30 minutes longer or until golden brown and center is set.

In a small saucepan, combine sugar, cornstarch and water until smooth. Bring to a boil over medium heat; cook and stir for 3 minutes. Stir in blueberries; reduce heat. Simmer for 8-10 minutes or until berries have burst. Stir in butter until melted. Serve with French toast. **Yield:** 6-8 servings (1-3/4 cups sauce).

Spinach Feta Strata

Pat Lane, Pullman, Washington

This is a fairly new recipe for me and was shared by a friend. My family has loved it since the first time I made it.

       10 slices French bread (1 inch thick) *or* 6
          croissants, split
        6 eggs
    1-1/2 cups milk
        1 package (10 ounces) frozen chopped
          spinach, thawed and squeezed dry

Spinach Feta Strata

Sparkling Oranges

Make-Ahead Scrambled Eggs

Diane Sackfield, Kingston, Ontario

I've served this convenient dish for breakfast and also as part of a full brunch buffet alongside breads and fruit.

- 5 tablespoons butter, *divided*
- 1/4 cup all-purpose flour
- 2 cups milk
- 2 cups (8 ounces) shredded cheddar cheese
- 1 cup sliced fresh mushrooms
- 1/4 cup finely chopped onion
- 12 eggs, beaten
- 1 teaspoon salt
- 1 package (10 ounces) frozen chopped broccoli, cooked and drained
- 1 cup soft bread crumbs

In a saucepan, melt 2 tablespoons butter. Add flour; cook and stir until the mixture begins to bubble. Gradually stir in milk; bring to boil. Cook and stir for 2 minutes. Remove from the heat.

Stir in cheese until melted; set aside. In a large skillet, saute mushrooms and onion in 2 tablespoons butter until tender. Add eggs and salt; cook and stir until the eggs are completely set. Add the cheese sauce and broccoli; mix well.

Pour into a greased 11-in. x 7-in. x 2-in. baking dish. Melt the remaining butter and toss with bread crumbs. Sprinkle over egg mixture. Cover and refrigerate overnight.

Remove from the refrigerator 30 minutes before baking. Bake, uncovered, at 350° for 25-30 minutes or until top is golden brown. **Yield:** 6-8 servings.

- 1/2 teaspoon salt
- 1/4 teaspoon ground nutmeg
- 1/4 teaspoon pepper
- 1-1/2 cups (6 ounces) shredded Monterey Jack cheese
- 1 cup (4 ounces) crumbled feta cheese

In a greased 13-in. x 9-in. x 2-in. baking dish, arrange French bread or croissant halves with sides overlapping.

In a large bowl, combine the eggs, milk, spinach, salt, nutmeg and pepper; pour over bread. Sprinkle with cheeses. Cover and refrigerate for 8 hours or overnight.

Remove from the refrigerator 30 minutes before baking. Bake, uncovered, at 350° for 40-45 minutes or until lightly browned. Serve warm. **Yield:** 12 servings.

Sparkling Oranges

Janie Bush, Weskan, Kansas

When I found the recipe for this simple yet elegant medley, I was thrilled because we had a surplus of fresh oranges!

- 8 large oranges, peeled and sectioned
- 1/2 cup sugar
- 1/2 cup orange marmalade
- 1 cup white grape juice
- 1/2 cup lemon-lime soda
- 3 tablespoons slivered almonds, toasted
- 3 tablespoons flaked coconut, toasted

Place orange sections in a large bowl. In a saucepan, combine sugar and marmalade; cook and stir over medium heat until sugar is dissolved. Remove from heat.

Stir in grape juice and soda. Pour over oranges and toss to coat. Cover and refrigerate overnight. Using a slotted spoon, remove oranges to a serving dish. Sprinkle with almonds and coconut. **Yield:** 8 servings.

Make-Ahead Scrambled Eggs

Brunch Enchiladas

cheese; bake 3 minutes longer or until the cheese is melted. Let stand for 10 minutes before serving. **Yield:** 10 enchiladas.

Nutrition Facts: One enchilada (prepared with reduced-fat ham, fat-free flour tortillas, reduced-fat cheddar cheese, fat-free milk and egg substitute equivalent to 6 eggs) equals 236 calories, 4 g fat (0 saturated fat), 18 mg cholesterol, 791 mg sodium, 28 g carbohydrate, 0 fiber, 20 g protein. **Diabetic Exchanges:** 2 starch, 2 lean meat.

Fruit 'n' Oat Yogurt

Susanne Melton, Mission Viejo, California

This combination of yogurt, oats, fruit and nuts is a delightful alternative to standard oatmeal. After sampling this yummy treat at my sister's, I just had to have the recipe.

 Uses less fat, sugar or salt. Includes Nutrition Facts.

- 2 cups (16 ounces) fat-free vanilla yogurt
- 1 cup quick-cooking oats
- 1 can (8 ounces) crushed pineapple, undrained
- 1/2 cup slivered almonds, toasted
- 2 medium firm bananas, sliced

In a bowl, combine the yogurt, oats, pineapple and almonds; cover and refrigerate overnight. Serve with sliced bananas. **Yield:** 4 servings.

Nutrition Facts: 3/4 cup equals 370 calories, 10 g fat (1 g saturated fat), 2 mg cholesterol, 85 mg sodium, 58 g carbohydrate, 5 g fiber, 13 g protein.

Ham Floret Strata

Elizabeth Montgomery, Taylorville, Illinois

It's a cinch to prepare this fluffy egg casserole the night before using frozen vegetables. In the morning, the aroma is wonderful while it bakes.

- 2 cups frozen broccoli florets
- 2 cups frozen cauliflowerets
- 1 cup cubed fully cooked ham
- 8 slices bread, crusts removed and cubed
- 8 eggs
- 1-1/2 cups milk
- 1 to 2 teaspoons ground mustard
- 1/4 to 1/2 teaspoon garlic powder
- 1/4 to 1/2 teaspoon onion powder
- 1-1/2 cups (6 ounces) shredded cheddar cheese

Place the broccoli and cauliflower in a greased 13-in. x 9-in. x 2-in. baking dish. Top with ham and bread. In a bowl, beat eggs, milk, mustard, garlic powder and onion powder. Pour over bread. Sprinkle with cheese. Cover and refrigerate for 8 hours or overnight.

Brunch Enchiladas

Gail Sykora, Menomonee Falls, Wisconsin

When I'm expecting company for brunch, the menu often includes this tried-and-true dish. The hearty enchiladas are filled with ham, eggs and plenty of cheese.

 Uses less fat, sugar or salt. Includes Nutrition Facts and Diabetic Exchanges.

- 2 cups cubed fully cooked ham
- 1/2 cup chopped green onions
- 10 flour tortillas (8 inches)
- 2 cups (8 ounces) shredded cheddar cheese, *divided*
- 1 tablespoon all-purpose flour
- 2 cups half-and-half cream
- 6 eggs, beaten
- 1/4 teaspoon salt, optional

Combine ham and onions; place about 1/3 cup down the center of each tortilla. Top with 2 tablespoons cheese. Roll up and place seam side down in a greased 13-in. x 9-in. x 2-in. baking dish.

In a bowl, combine flour, cream, eggs and salt if desired until smooth. Pour over tortillas. Cover and refrigerate for 8 hours or overnight.

Remove from the refrigerator 30 minutes before baking. Cover and bake at 350° for 25 minutes. Uncover; bake for 10 minutes. Sprinkle with remaining

Remove from the refrigerator 30 minutes before baking. Bake, uncovered, at 350° for 40-50 minutes or until a knife inserted near the center comes out clean. Let stand 10 minutes before serving. **Yield:** 8 servings.

Cranberry Slush Punch

Martha Artyomenko, Libby, Montana

With ruby-red color and a tangy taste, this festive drink is always a hit at Christmastime. We also served it at my sister's wedding, and guests told us it was some of the best punch they'd ever tasted! The combination of the frosty cranberry mixture and lemon-lime soda is hard to beat.

- 3 **cans (8 ounces** *each***) jellied cranberry sauce**
- 2 **cans (12 ounces** *each***) lemonade concentrate**
- 1 **can (12 ounces) frozen cranberry-apple juice concentrate**
- 4 **cups water**
- 1 **teaspoon ground cinnamon**
- 1/2 **teaspoon ground allspice**
- 12 **cups lemon-lime soda, chilled**

In a bowl, combine the cranberry sauce, lemonade concentrate, cranberry-apple juice concentrate, water, cinnamon and allspice. Cover and freeze for 8 hours or overnight.

Remove slush mixture from the freezer 45 minutes before serving. For each serving, combine 1/2 cup slush mixture with 1/2 cup lemon-lime soda. **Yield:** 24 servings (1 cup each).

Cranberry Slush Punch

Baked Brunch Sandwiches

Baked Brunch Sandwiches

Carolyn Herfkens, Crysler, Ontario

Serving brunch to your bunch is a breeze when you prepare these convenient sandwiches the night before. You just store them in the refrigerator overnight, then pop them in the oven in the morning! The sandwiches combine the flavor of grilled ham and cheese with the puffy texture of French toast.

- 3 **tablespoons Dijon mustard**
- 12 **slices bread**
- 6 **slices fully cooked ham**
- 12 **slices cheddar** *or* **Swiss cheese**
- 1 **medium tomato, thinly sliced**
- 3 **tablespoons butter, softened**
- 4 **eggs**
- 1/4 **cup milk**
- 1/4 **teaspoon pepper**

Spread mustard on one side of six slices of bread. Layer ham, cheese and tomato over mustard; top with remaining bread. Butter the outsides of the sandwiches; cut in half.

Arrange the cut sandwiches in a greased 13-in. x 9-in. x 2-in. baking dish. Beat the eggs, milk and pepper; pour over sandwiches. Cover and refrigerate sandwiches overnight.

Remove from the refrigerator 30 minutes before baking. Bake, uncovered, at 375° for 30 minutes or until the sandwiches are golden brown and the cheese is melted. **Yield:** 6 servings.

Zesty Breakfast Burritos

Breakfast Bread Pudding

Alma Andrews, Live Oak, Florida

I like to assemble this comforting, old-fashioned dish the day before our grandchildren visit. It gives me more time for fun with them!

- 12 slices white bread
- 1 package (8 ounces) cream cheese, cubed
- 12 eggs
- 2 cups milk
- 1/3 cup maple syrup
- 1/4 teaspoon salt

Remove and discard crusts from bread; cut bread into cubes. Toss lightly with cream cheese cubes; place in a greased 13-in. x 9-in. x 2-in. baking pan. In a large mixing bowl, beat eggs. Add milk, syrup and salt; mix well. Pour over bread mixture. Cover and refrigerate 8 hours or overnight.

Remove from refrigerator 30 minutes before baking. Bake, uncovered, at 375° for 40-45 minutes or until a knife inserted near the center comes out clean. Let stand 5 minutes before cutting. **Yield:** 6-8 servings.

Nutty French Toast

Mavis Diment, Marcus, Iowa

This tempting treat is a cross between two breakfast favorites—gooey caramel rolls and French toast. No one can resist that sweet combination!

- 12 slices French bread (1 inch thick)
- 8 eggs
- 2 cups milk
- 2 teaspoons vanilla extract
- 1/2 teaspoon ground cinnamon
- 3/4 cup butter, softened

Nutty French Toast

Zesty Breakfast Burritos

Angie Ibarra, Stillwater, Minnesota

My husband grew up in Mexico and prefers his food extra spicy. Chili powder and other seasonings added to the ground pork give these sausage-and-egg wraps a nice kick.

- 1 pound ground pork
- 2 tablespoons white vinegar
- 1 tablespoon chili powder
- 1 teaspoon dried oregano
- 1 teaspoon salt
- 1 garlic clove, minced
- 6 eggs
- 1/4 cup milk
- 1 tablespoon vegetable oil
- 6 flour tortillas (8 inches), warmed

Taco sauce

Combine pork, vinegar, chili powder, oregano, salt and garlic; mix well. Cover and chill overnight.

In a skillet over medium heat, cook pork mixture until no longer pink. Drain; keep warm. Beat eggs and milk. In another skillet, heat oil. Cook eggs over low heat until set, stirring occasionally. Spoon about 1/4 cup pork mixture and 1/4 cup eggs down the center of each tortilla. Top with taco sauce and roll up. **Yield:** 6 servings.

1-1/3 cups packed brown sugar
   3 tablespoons dark corn syrup
   1 cup chopped walnuts

Place bread in a greased 13-in. x 9-in. x 2-in. baking dish. In a large bowl, beat eggs, milk, vanilla and cinnamon; pour over the bread. Cover and refrigerate overnight. Remove from the refrigerator 30 minutes before baking.

Meanwhile, in a mixing bowl, cream butter, brown sugar and syrup until smooth; spread over bread. Sprinkle with nuts. Bake, uncovered, at 350° for 1 hour or until golden brown. **Yield:** 6-8 servings.

Overnight Yeast Waffles

Mary Balcomb, Crooked River Ranch, Oregon

These golden waffles are crispy on the outside and tender on the inside. They're so good, I'll even freeze a batch so I can have them for breakfast on extra-busy mornings.

   1 package (1/4 ounce) active dry yeast
1/2 cup warm water (110° to 115°)
   1 teaspoon sugar
   2 cups warm milk (110° to 115°)
1/2 cup butter, melted
   2 eggs, lightly beaten
   2 cups all-purpose flour
   1 teaspoon salt

In a large mixing bowl, dissolve the yeast in warm water. Add the sugar; let stand for 5 minutes. Add the milk, butter and eggs; mix well. Combine the flour and salt; stir into the milk mixture. Cover and refrigerate the batter overnight.

Stir batter. For each waffle, pour by 1/4 cupfuls into a preheated waffle iron; bake according to manufacturer's directions until golden brown. **Yield:** 10 servings.

Pork Sausage Puff

Christina French, Elkhart, Indiana

A dear lady at our church shared this recipe with me. I altered the ingredients a bit to suit my family's tastes, and it became an instant favorite.

   1 cup biscuit/baking mix
   6 eggs, beaten
   2 cups milk
2-1/2 cups cooked bulk pork sausage (1 pound uncooked)
   1 cup (4 ounces) shredded cheddar cheese
1/2 teaspoon dried oregano

In a bowl, combine the biscuit mix, eggs and milk until blended. Add the cooked sausage, cheese and oregano.

Transfer to a greased 13-in. x 9-in. x 2-in. baking dish.

Reuben Brunch Bake

Cover and refrigerate overnight. Or bake, uncovered, at 350° for 50-55 minutes or until a knife inserted near the center comes out clean. If refrigerated before baking, remove from the refrigerator 30 minutes beforehand. **Yield:** 6 servings.

Reuben Brunch Bake

Janelle Reed, Merriam, Kansas

I came up with this when I wanted something different for a graduation brunch for two of our sons. When I realized I had most of the ingredients on hand for the reuben dip I usually make, I decided to use them in a casserole instead. Everyone asked for the recipe!

   8 eggs, lightly beaten
   1 can (14-1/2 ounces) sauerkraut, rinsed and well drained
   2 cups (8 ounces) shredded Swiss cheese
   1 package (2-1/2 ounces) deli corned beef, cut into 1-inch pieces
1/2 cup chopped green onions
1/2 cup milk
   1 tablespoon Dijon mustard
1/4 teaspoon salt
1/4 teaspoon pepper
   3 slices rye bread, toasted and coarsely chopped
1/4 cup butter, melted

In a large bowl, combine the first nine ingredients. Pour into a greased 11-in. x 7-in. x 2-in. baking dish. Cover and refrigerate overnight.

Remove from the refrigerator 30 minutes before baking. Toss bread crumbs and butter; sprinkle over casserole. Bake, uncovered, at 350° for 40-45 minutes or until a knife inserted near the center comes out clean. Let stand for 10 minutes before serving. **Yield:** 8-12 servings.

Cherry Almond Pull-Apart Bread

Georgina Edwards, Kelowna, British Columbia

These yummy, gooey rolls are wonderful for holiday mornings or any time you have guests for breakfast. When my son and son-in-law visit, they devour these treats almost as soon as they hit the table. The recipe uses convenient frozen dough but still delivers from-scratch taste.

       6 tablespoons butter, melted, *divided*
   1/2 cup sugar
       3 teaspoons ground cinnamon
     20 frozen bread dough dinner rolls
   1/2 cup sliced almonds, toasted
   1/2 cup candied cherries, halved
   1/3 cup corn syrup

Place 3 tablespoons butter in a small bowl. In another bowl, combine the sugar and cinnamon. Dip 10 frozen dough rolls in butter, then roll in cinnamon-sugar. Place in a greased 10-in. fluted tube pan. Sprinkle with half of the almonds and candied cherries.

Repeat with the remaining rolls, almonds and candied cherries. Combine the corn syrup and remaining butter; pour over the cherries. Cover and refrigerate the bread overnight.

Remove from the refrigerator. Cover and let rise until almost doubled, about 2 hours. Bake at 350° for 30-35 minutes or until golden brown. Immediately invert onto a serving plate. Serve warm. **Yield:** 20 servings.

Cherry Almond Pull-Apart Bread

Maple French Toast Casserole

Melissa Faye Paxton, Clifton Forge, Virginia

When I first served this casserole to family visiting from California, they all wanted the recipe. I'd never had so many compliments on my cooking before!

       7 cups cubed French bread
   1/2 cup golden raisins
       1 package (3 ounces) cream cheese, softened
       1 cup warm heavy whipping cream (70° to 80°)
   1/4 cup maple syrup
       6 eggs
   1/2 teaspoon vanilla extract
   1/4 teaspoon ground cinnamon
   1/8 teaspoon salt
Additional maple syrup

Place bread in a greased 2-qt. baking dish; press down gently. Sprinkle with raisins. In a small mixing bowl, beat the cream cheese until fluffy. Gradually beat in whipping cream and syrup; mix well.

Whisk together the eggs, vanilla, cinnamon and salt; add to cream cheese mixture. Pour evenly over bread; lightly press bread into egg mixture with a spatula. Cover; refrigerate for 8 hours or overnight.

Remove from the refrigerator 30 minutes before baking. Cover and bake at 375° for 25 minutes. Uncover; bake 20-25 minutes longer or until center is set and the top is golden brown. Serve with syrup. **Yield:** 6 servings.

Picante Potato Pie

Janet Hill, Sacramento, California

This bacon-topped pie is a tasty and convenient addition to brunch menus. It's one of my top choices for breakfast when I have overnight guests.

       5 eggs
2-1/2 cups frozen shredded hash brown potatoes
       1 cup (4 ounces) shredded Monterey Jack cheese
   1/2 cup shredded sharp cheddar cheese
   2/3 cup picante sauce
       2 green onions, sliced
   1/4 teaspoon salt
       6 bacon strips, cooked and crumbled
Additional picante sauce, optional

In a bowl, beat eggs. Stir in the hash browns, cheese, picante sauce, onions and salt. Pour into a greased 9-in. pie plate. Cover and refrigerate overnight.

Remove from the refrigerator 30 minutes before baking. Bake at 350° for 25 minutes. Sprinkle with bacon; bake 5-10 minutes longer or until a knife inserted near the center comes out clean. Serve with additional picante sauce if desired. **Yield:** 6 servings.

Hash Brown Egg Bake

Hash Brown Egg Bake

Cheryl Johnson, Plymouth, Minnesota

A package of frozen hash browns makes this recipe simple to prepare. With bacon and cheddar cheese, it's a sure winner for breakfast, brunch and even dinner.

    1 package (32 ounces) frozen cubed hash
       brown potatoes, thawed
    1 pound sliced bacon, cooked and crumbled
    1 cup (4 ounces) shredded cheddar cheese,
       divided
 1/4 to 1/2 teaspoon salt
    8 eggs
    2 cups milk
Dash paprika

In a large bowl, combine the hash browns, bacon, 1/2 cup cheese and salt. Spoon into a greased 13-in. x 9-in. x 2-in. baking dish. In a bowl, beat the eggs and milk until smooth; pour over the hash brown mixture. Sprinkle with paprika.

Cover and refrigerate overnight. Or bake, uncovered, at 350° for 45-50 minutes until golden. Top with the remaining cheese. If refrigerated before baking, remove from the refrigerator 30 minutes beforehand. **Yield:** 8 servings.

A Good Egg

When buying eggs, look for shells that are clean and unbroken. Store eggs in the carton or the egg compartment in the refrigerator and use them by the expiration date.

Apple Waffle Grills (p. 54)

Best of Country Breakfast & Brunch

Chapter 4

Breakfasts To Go

Is time too tight for a sit-down breakfast? These handheld standbys are easy to munch on the run…just grab one and go!

Confetti Scrambled Egg Pockets

Confetti Scrambled Egg Pockets

Dixie Terry, Goreville, Illinois

I like to make these grab-and-go pockets on busy mornings and even with a light salad for supper. The egg-packed pitas are colorful and always satisfying.

✓ **Uses less fat, sugar or salt. Includes Nutrition Facts and Diabetic Exchanges.**

    1 **cup fresh *or* frozen corn**
 1/4 **cup chopped green pepper**
    2 **tablespoons chopped onion**
    1 **jar (2 ounces) diced pimientos, drained**
    1 **tablespoon butter**
1-1/4 **cups egg substitute**
    3 **eggs**
 1/4 **cup fat-free evaporated milk**
 1/2 **teaspoon seasoned salt**
    1 **medium tomato, seeded and chopped**
    1 **green onion, sliced**
    3 **whole wheat pita breads (6 inches), halved**

In a large nonstick skillet, saute the corn, green pepper, onion and pimientos in butter for 5-7 minutes or until tender. Combine the egg substitute, eggs, milk and salt; pour into skillet. Cook and stir over medium heat until eggs are completely set. Stir in the tomato and green onion. Spoon about 2/3 cup into each pita half. **Yield:** 6 servings.

    Nutrition Facts: One serving (1 filled pita half) equals 207 calories, 6 g fat (2 g saturated fat), 112 mg cholesterol, 538 mg sodium, 28 g carbohydrate, 4 g fiber, 13 g protein. **Diabetic Exchanges:** 1-1/2 starch, 1 lean meat, 1 vegetable, 1/2 fat.

French Toast Sandwiches

Eleanor Smith, Hot Springs Village, Arkansas

The popular combination of peanut butter and banana gives this French toast a fun twist. I've found that both kids and adults enjoy these scrumptious sandwiches.

1/4 **cup peanut butter**
  4 **slices whole wheat bread**
  1 **small firm banana, sliced**
  2 **eggs**
1/3 **cup milk**

1/4 teaspoon ground cinnamon
1/4 teaspoon vanilla extract
1 tablespoon butter
Honey, optional

Spread peanut butter on two slices of bread. Top with banana slices and remaining bread. In a shallow bowl, whisk the eggs, milk, cinnamon and vanilla. Dip both sides of sandwiches into egg mixture.

In a large skillet, melt butter over medium heat; grill sandwiches on both sides until golden brown. Serve with honey if desired. **Yield:** 2 servings.

Strawberry Oatmeal Bars

Flo Burtnett, Gage, Oklahoma

A yummy strawberry filling and fluffy coconut topping make these oatmeal bars irresistible. They're a sweet way to start out your day...and are a nice addition to your cookie tray at Christmastime, too.

1-1/4 cups all-purpose flour
1-1/4 cups quick-cooking oats
1/2 cup sugar
1/2 teaspoon baking powder
1/4 teaspoon salt
3/4 cup butter, melted
2 teaspoons vanilla extract
1 cup strawberry preserves
1/2 cup flaked coconut

In a bowl, combine dry ingredients. Add butter and vanilla; stir until crumbly. Set aside 1 cup. Press remaining crumb mixture evenly into an ungreased 13-in. x 9-in. x 2-in. baking pan. Spread preserves over crust. Combine coconut and reserved crumb mixture; sprin-

Mini Mexican Quiches

kle over preserves.

Bake at 350° for 25-30 minutes or until coconut is lightly browned. Cool. **Yield:** 3 dozen.

Mini Mexican Quiches

Linda Hendrix, Moundville, Missouri

With south-of-the-border flavor, these fun finger foods are delicious not only for breakfast or brunch but also as appetizers for parties.

1/2 cup butter, softened
1 package (3 ounces) cream cheese, softened
1 cup all-purpose flour
1 cup (4 ounces) shredded Monterey Jack cheese
1 can (4 ounces) chopped green chilies, drained
2 eggs
1/2 cup heavy whipping cream
1/4 teaspoon salt
1/8 teaspoon pepper

In a small mixing bowl, cream butter and cream cheese. Add flour; beat until well blended. Shape into 24 balls; cover and refrigerate for 1 hour.

Press balls onto the bottom and up the sides of greased miniature muffin cups. Sprinkle a rounded teaspoonful of cheese and 1/2 teaspoon of chilies into each shell. In a bowl, beat eggs, cream, salt and pepper. Spoon into shells.

Bake at 350° for 30-35 minutes or until golden brown. Let stand for 5 minutes before serving. Refrigerate leftovers. **Yield:** 2 dozen.

Strawberry Oatmeal Bars

Bacon Avocado Burritos

Cleo Gossett, Ephrata, Washington

The tortillas for these burritos are dipped in beaten eggs and cooked to give them color and flavor. I set out a variety of filling ingredients and toppings, then let everyone assemble their own.

    4 eggs
    8 flour tortillas (7 inches)
    1 to 2 tablespoons vegetable oil
1-1/2 cups (6 ounces) shredded cheddar cheese
    1 large ripe avocado, thinly sliced
1-1/2 cups chopped green onions
    1 pound sliced bacon, cooked and crumbled
Salsa, ranch salad dressing *or* sour cream

In a bowl, beat the eggs. Dip one tortilla in eggs. In a large skillet, cook tortilla in oil just until egg sets; turn to cook other side. Remove and place between paper towels to drain; keep warm. Repeat with remaining tortillas, adding more oil if needed.

Place cheese, avocado, onions and bacon down the center of tortillas; top with salsa, salad dressing or sour cream. Fold ends and sides over filling. If desired, filled burritos may be warmed in the microwave just before serving. **Yield:** 8 servings.

Bacon Avocado Burritos

Sausage Egg Subs

Dee Pasternak, Bristol, Indiana

Spicy chunks of sausage give winning flavor to this scrambled egg mixture. Served on a bun, it makes a satisfying, all-in-one sandwich that people enjoy any time of day.

Sausage Egg Subs

1-1/4 pounds bulk pork sausage
    1/4 cup chopped onion
    12 eggs, lightly beaten
    1/2 cup chopped fresh mushrooms
    1 to 2 tablespoons finely chopped green pepper
    1 to 2 tablespoons finely chopped sweet red pepper
    6 submarine sandwich buns (about 6 inches), split

In a large skillet over medium heat, cook sausage and onion until the meat is no longer pink; drain. Remove with a slotted spoon and keep warm. In the same skillet, cook and stir the eggs until nearly set, about 7 minutes. Add mushrooms, peppers and the sausage mixture. Cook until eggs are completely set and mixture is heated through. Serve on buns. **Yield:** 6 servings.

Take-Along Raisin Squares

Shirley A. Glaab, Hattiesburg, Mississippi

Loaded with raisins, dates, chocolate chips and almonds, these moist bars are perfect to grab when you're dashing out the door in the morning. But they're nice to take along on just about any outing.

    1/2 cup butter, softened
    3/4 cup packed brown sugar

1 egg
1 teaspoon vanilla extract
1 cup old-fashioned oats
1/2 cup all-purpose flour
1-1/4 cups raisins
1 cup chopped almonds
1 cup chopped dates
1/2 cup semisweet chocolate chips
2 tablespoons All-Bran, optional

In a small mixing bowl, cream butter and brown sugar until light and fluffy. Beat in the egg and vanilla. Gradually add oats and flour. Stir in the raisins, almonds, dates and chocolate chips (batter will be thick).

Spread into a greased 8-in. square baking dish. Sprinkle with bran if desired. Bake at 350° for 20-25 minutes or until toothpick inserted near the center comes out clean. Cool completely on a wire rack. Cut into squares. **Yield:** 12 servings.

Mini Apricot Turnovers

These warm-from-the-oven goodies prove that turnovers don't have to be time-consuming to prepare. The Taste of Home Test Kitchen staff created them with purchased pie pastry and fruit preserves.

1 package (15 ounces) refrigerated pie pastry
1 jar (12 ounces) apricot *or* peach preserves
2 tablespoons milk
1 tablespoon sugar
1/4 teaspoon ground cinnamon

Mini Apricot Turnovers

Sausage Cheese Puffs

Cut each pastry into four wedges. Place a rounded tablespoonful of preserves in the center of each. Moisten edges with water. Fold pastry over filling; press edges with fork to seal.

Place turnovers on an ungreased baking sheet. Cut a small slit in the top of each. Brush with milk. Combine sugar and cinnamon; sprinkle over turnovers. Bake at 425° for 16-18 minutes or until golden brown. Serve warm. **Yield:** 8 turnovers.

Sausage Cheese Puffs

Della Moore, Troy, New York

People are surprised when I tell them these bite-size puffs have only four ingredients. Cheesy and spicy, the golden morsels are terrific for a quick breakfast and can even make great appetizers.

1 pound bulk Italian sausage
3 cups biscuit/baking mix
4 cups (16 ounces) shredded cheddar cheese
3/4 cup water

In a skillet, cook and crumble sausage until no longer pink; drain. In a bowl, combine biscuit mix and cheese; stir in sausage. Add water and toss with a fork until moistened. Shape into 1-1/2-in. balls. Place 2 in. apart on ungreased baking sheets. Bake at 400° for 12-15 minutes or until puffed and golden brown. Cool on wire racks. **Yield:** about 4 dozen.

Editor's Note: Baked puffs may be frozen; reheat at 400° for 7-9 minutes or until heated through (they do not need to be thawed first).

Ham Muffinwiches

Ham Muffinwiches

Jenny Wiebe, Villa Hills, Kentucky

I came up with these hearty bites when I needed something to pack for lunch. The tender muffins freeze well and are perfect to take on your way out in the morning, too.

    1 package (8-1/2 ounces) corn bread/muffin
       mix
1/8 teaspoon ground mustard
1/3 cup milk
    1 tablespoon vegetable oil
    1 egg
    1 cup chopped fully cooked ham
1/4 cup thinly sliced green onions
    2 tablespoons shredded cheddar cheese

In a bowl, combine corn bread mix, mustard, milk, oil and egg just until blended. Stir in the ham and onions.

Fill greased or paper-lined muffin cups half full. Bake at 400° for 15-20 minutes or until a toothpick comes out clean. Immediately sprinkle with cheese. Cool for 5 minutes before removing from pan. Serve warm. **Yield:** 9 muffins.

Apple Waffle Grills

(Pictured on page 48)

Sonia Daily, Warren, Michigan

These quick and easy breakfast sandwiches are also great later in the day. My husband likes them best when I add a slice of ham between the waffles.

    4 teaspoons butter
    4 frozen waffles, thawed
    4 slices process American cheese
    1 medium tart apple, thinly sliced

In a large skillet, melt butter over medium heat. Add two waffles; top each with one cheese slice, apple slices, and remaining cheese and waffles. Cook until waffles are lightly toasted on both sides and cheese is melted. **Yield:** 2 servings.

Bacon Buns

Mary Ann Simkus, Hampshire, Illinois

These stuffed rolls are a family tradition. If you like, replace the bacon in the filling with ground cooked ham.

  10 bacon strips, diced
1/3 cup chopped onion
    1 package (16 ounces) hot roll mix
    1 egg, lightly beaten

For bacon filling, in a skillet, cook bacon and onion over medium heat until bacon is crisp and onion is tender; drain on paper towels.

Prepare hot roll mix according to package directions. Turn the dough onto a floured surface; knead until smooth and elastic, about 5 minutes. Place in a greased bowl, turning once to grease top. Cover and let rise in a warm place until doubled, about 40 minutes.

Divide dough into 18 pieces. On a floured surface, roll out each into a 5-in. circle. Top each with 1 tablespoon of filling. Fold dough around filling, shaping each piece into a small loaf; pinch edges to seal. Place seam side down on greased baking sheets. Cover loosely with plastic wrap coated with nonstick cooking spray. Let rise in a warm place for 20-30 minutes.

Brush egg over buns. Bake at 350° for 20-25 minutes or until golden brown. Remove from pans to wire racks. Serve warm. Refrigerate leftovers. **Yield:** 1-1/2 dozen.

Bacon Buns

Bacon 'n' Egg Sandwiches

Ann Fuemmeler, Glasgow, Missouri

I came across this unique grilled combo while digging in my mom's recipe box. I'm glad I did!

- 1/2 cup sour cream
- 8 slices bread
- 4 green onions, chopped
- 4 slices process American cheese
- 2 hard-cooked eggs, cut into 1/4-inch slices
- 8 bacon strips, cooked and drained
- 1/4 cup butter, softened

Spread sour cream on one side of four slices of bread. Top with onions, cheese, eggs and bacon. Top with the remaining bread. Butter outsides of sandwiches; cook in a large skillet over medium heat until golden brown on both sides. **Yield:** 4 servings.

Vegetarian Burritos

Ruth Behm, Defiance, Ohio

Our daughter loves to help me out in the kitchen. We use just six ingredients, including convenient salsa, to create the zippy filling in these burritos.

☑ **Uses less fat, sugar or salt. Includes Nutrition Facts and Diabetic Exchanges.**

- 10 eggs
- 1/2 teaspoon salt, optional
- 1/8 teaspoon pepper

- 1 cup salsa
- 1/4 cup chopped onion
- 1 cup (4 ounces) shredded cheddar cheese
- 8 flour tortillas (6 to 7 inches), warmed

In a bowl, beat the eggs, salt if desired and pepper. Pour into a skillet that has been coated with nonstick cooking spray. Cook and stir over medium heat until eggs are partially set.

Add salsa and onion; cook and stir until eggs are completely set. Sprinkle with cheese. Spoon about 1/2 cup down the center of each tortilla; fold ends and sides over filling. Serve immediately. **Yield:** 8 servings.

Nutrition Facts: One serving (prepared with egg substitute, reduced-fat cheese and fat-free tortillas and without salt) equals 240 calories, 7 g fat (0 saturated fat), 269 mg cholesterol, 826 mg sodium, 27 g carbohydrate, 0 fiber, 14 g protein. **Diabetic Exchanges:** 1-1/2 starch, 1 meat, 1 vegetable, 1/2 fat.

Eggshell Ease

Planning to make delicious Bacon 'n' Egg Sandwiches (on this page)? Consider buying the eggs several days before hard-cooking them—they'll be easier to peel.

White Chocolate Cranberry Granola Bars

White Chocolate Cranberry Granola Bars

Janis Loomis, Madison, Virginia

I created these chewy, chock-full treats when I was searching for a healthy snack for my family. Now the bars are one of my most-requested recipes.

☑ **Uses less fat, sugar or salt. Includes Nutrition Facts and Diabetic Exchanges.**

- 1/4 cup sugar
- 1/4 cup maple syrup
- 1/4 cup honey
- 2 tablespoons reduced-fat peanut butter
- 1 egg white
- 1 tablespoon fat-free evaporated milk
- 1 teaspoon vanilla extract
- 1 cup whole wheat flour
- 1/2 teaspoon baking soda
- 1/2 teaspoon ground cinnamon
- 1/4 teaspoon ground allspice
- 2 cups old-fashioned oats
- 1-1/2 cups crisp rice cereal
- 1/3 cup vanilla *or* white chips
- 1/4 cup dried cranberries
- 1/4 cup chopped walnuts

In a large bowl, combine the first seven ingredients; mix well. Combine the flour, baking soda, cinnamon and allspice; add to the sugar mixture. Stir in the remaining ingredients.

Press into a 13-in. x 9-in. x 2-in. baking pan coated with nonstick cooking spray. Bake at 350° for 18-20 minutes or until golden brown. Score the surface with shallow cuts, making rectangular bars. Cool completely on a wire rack. Cut along score lines. **Yield:** 2 dozen.

Nutrition Facts: One bar equals 109 calories, 3 g fat (1 g saturated fat), 1 mg cholesterol, 57 mg sodium, 20 g carbohydrate, 2 g fiber, 3 g protein. **Diabetic Exchange:** 1-1/2 starch.

Smoked Sausage Pockets

Jan Badovinac, Harrison, Arkansas

These golden, oven-baked bundles have a complete breakfast hidden inside—whole sausage links, scrambled eggs and a cheesy seasoned spread. Using refrigerated biscuit dough speeds up the preparation.

- 2 packages (3 ounces *each*) cream cheese, softened
- 1-1/2 teaspoons minced fresh parsley
- 3/4 teaspoon seasoned salt
- 1/4 teaspoon pepper
- 2/3 cup shredded cheddar cheese
- 2 tablespoons butter
- 5 eggs, beaten
- 1 tube (17.3 ounces) large refrigerated biscuits
- 1 egg white
- 1 teaspoon water
- 16 miniature smoked sausage links

In a mixing bowl, combine the cream cheese, parsley, seasoned salt and pepper. Stir in the cheddar cheese; set aside. In a skillet, melt the butter over medium heat. Add beaten eggs; cook and stir until completely set.

Separate the refrigerated biscuits into eight pieces. On a lightly floured surface, roll each biscuit piece into a 5-in. circle. On each circle, spread about 2 tablespoons of the cream cheese mixture to within 1/2 in. of the edges.

Beat egg white and water; lightly brush some over edges of dough. Top with scrambled eggs and two sausage links. Fold dough over; seal edges and press together with a fork.

Place on an ungreased baking sheet. Brush with remaining egg white mixture. Bake at 375° for 14-16 minutes or until golden brown. **Yield:** 8 servings.

Breakfast Bars

Candace Jenks, Minot, North Dakota

I like to bake a batch of these not-too-sweet squares and stash any extras in the freezer. When I need a quick breakfast or afternoon snack, I just thaw the bars in the microwave and enjoy.

- 1 cup butter, softened
- 1 cup packed brown sugar
- 1 cup quick-cooking oats
- 1 cup all-purpose flour
- 1 cup whole wheat flour
- 1/2 cup toasted wheat germ
- 4 eggs
- 2 cups chopped pecans
- 1 cup flaked coconut
- 1 cup (6 ounces) semisweet chocolate chips

Bacon 'n' Egg Biscuits

In a mixing bowl, cream the butter and brown sugar. Combine the oats, all-purpose flour, whole wheat flour and wheat germ; gradually add to creamed mixture. Press into a greased 13-in. x 9-in. x 2-in. baking pan. In a small bowl, beat the eggs until foamy. Stir in the chopped pecans, coconut and chocolate chips. Spread evenly over the crust.

Bake at 350° for 30-35 minutes or until edges are golden brown. Cool on a wire rack. Cut into bars. Store in the refrigerator. **Yield:** about 2 dozen.

Bacon 'n' Egg Biscuits

Katie Koziolek, Hartland, Minnesota

These are great for busy mornings—the sandwiches go together in about 15 minutes when I use Buttermilk Biscuit Mix (recipe at right). While the flaky biscuits bake, I cook the eggs and warm up precooked bacon. Then I just add some cheese for a satisfying, homemade meal.

    2 cups Buttermilk Biscuit Mix (recipe at right)
    7 tablespoons water
    8 eggs
    8 slices process American cheese
    8 bacon strips, halved and cooked

In a bowl, combine biscuit mix and water just until blended. Turn onto a lightly floured surface and knead 5 times. Roll out to 1/2-in. thickness; cut with a 3-in. biscuit cutter. Place on an ungreased baking sheet. Bake at 425° for 9-10 minutes or until golden brown. Meanwhile, scramble the eggs. Split the biscuits; fill each with a slice of cheese, scrambled egg and two bacon pieces. **Yield:** 8 servings.

Buttermilk Biscuit Mix

Katie Koziolek, Hartland, Minnesota

I stir up a big batch of this versatile biscuit mix to use in dozens of recipes, including Bacon 'n' Egg Biscuits (recipe at left). This mix is easy to make and so convenient to have on hand.

        8 cups all-purpose flour
    1-1/2 cups buttermilk blend powder
        4 tablespoons baking powder
        3 tablespoons sugar
        2 teaspoons salt
        2 teaspoons cream of tartar
        1 teaspoon baking soda
    2-1/3 cups shortening

In a bowl, combine the first seven ingredients; cut in the shortening until crumbly. Store in an airtight container in a cool dry place for up to 6 months. **Yield:** about 13-1/2 cups.

Jelly Pancake Sandwiches

Laura Muskopf, Wooster, Ohio

I don't care for syrup on pancakes, so I created this recipe. Add some peanut butter if you'd like heartier sandwiches.

- 2 cups biscuit/baking mix
- 1 teaspoon ground cinnamon
- 1/4 teaspoon salt
- 1 cup milk
- 2 eggs, beaten
- Strawberry jelly *or* jam

In a bowl, combine the biscuit mix, cinnamon and salt. Add milk and eggs; mix well.

Pour batter by 1/4 cupfuls onto a greased hot griddle. Turn when bubbles form on top of pancakes; cook until second side is golden brown. Spread half of the pancakes with jelly; top with remaining pancakes. **Yield:** 5 servings.

Sausage Breakfast Wraps

Ed Rysdyk Jr., Wyoming, Michigan

I love breakfast burritos and came up with this healthier version that's lower in fat and cholesterol.

☑ **Uses less fat, sugar or salt. Includes Nutrition Facts and Diabetic Exchanges.**

- 1 pound turkey Italian sausage links, casings removed
- 1 medium sweet red pepper, diced
- 1 small onion, diced
- 4 cartons (8 ounces *each*) frozen egg substitute, thawed
- 1 can (4 ounces) chopped green chilies
- 1 teaspoon chili powder

Sausage Breakfast Wraps

- 10 flour tortillas (8 inches), warmed
- 1-1/4 cups salsa

In a nonstick skillet, cook sausage over medium heat until no longer pink; drain. Transfer to a 13-in. x 9-in. x 2-in. baking dish coated with nonstick cooking spray. Sprinkle with red pepper and onion. Combine the egg substitute, green chilies and chili powder; pour over sausage mixture.

Bake, uncovered, at 350° for 30-35 minutes or until set. Break up sausage mixture with a spoon. Place 2/3 cup down the center of each tortilla; top with salsa. Fold one end over sausage mixture, then fold two sides over. **Yield:** 10 servings.

Nutrition Facts: One serving (1 breakfast wrap with 2 tablespoons salsa) equals 286 calories, 7 g fat (2 g saturated fat), 24 mg cholesterol, 980 mg sodium, 33 g carbohydrate, 1 g fiber, 21 g protein. **Diabetic Exchanges:** 2 starch, 2 lean meat, 1/2 fat.

Apple Sausage Pitas

Michelle Komaroski, Pueblo, Colorado

This is my favorite breakfast for family and guests. Only four ingredients are needed for these tasty sandwiches.

- 1 package (8 ounces) brown-and-serve sausage links, sliced
- 4 medium tart apples, peeled and thinly sliced
- 1/4 cup maple syrup
- 6 pita breads (6 inches), halved

In a skillet, cook sausage and apples until sausage is heated through and apples are tender. Add syrup; heat though. In a microwave, warm pitas on high for 20 seconds. Fill with the sausage mixture. **Yield:** 4 servings.

Maple-Granola Trail Mix

Malone Davidson, Landrum, South Carolina

This crunchy medley is a great pick-me-up any time of day. I like to sprinkle it over yogurt or pack it in a lunch box.

- 4 cups old-fashioned oats
- 1/2 cup vegetable oil
- 1/2 cup maple syrup
- 1/2 cup slivered almonds
- 3 teaspoons vanilla extract
- 1/2 teaspoon ground cinnamon
- 1/3 cup *each* dried cranberries, chopped dried apples and chopped dried apricots
- 1/4 cup milk chocolate chips
- 1/4 cup butterscotch chips

In a large bowl, combine the oats, oil, syrup, almonds, vanilla and cinnamon. Spread in a 15-in. x 10-in. x 1-in.

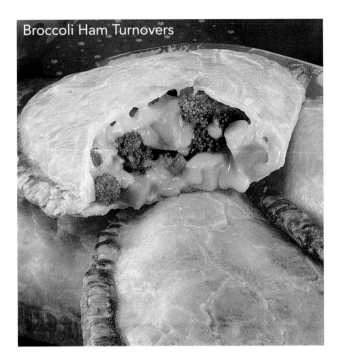
Broccoli Ham Turnovers

baking pan. Bake at 325° for 10-15 minutes. Stir; bake 20 minutes longer or until golden brown. Cool completely.

Add the dried fruit and chips; toss to combine. Store in an airtight container. **Yield:** about 6 cups.

Broccoli Ham Turnovers

Lupie Molinar, Tucson, Arizona

I'm always trying to come up with new and different dishes to serve family and friends. These savory, fresh-tasting turnovers were an instant hit.

    2 cups broccoli florets
1-1/2 cups (6 ounces) shredded sharp cheddar
      cheese
  1/2 cup cubed fully cooked ham
  1/2 cup sliced green onions
    1 tablespoon minced fresh parsley
  1/4 teaspoon ground nutmeg
Salt and pepper to taste
Pastry for double-crust pie
    1 egg
    1 tablespoon heavy whipping cream

Place broccoli in a steamer basket over 1 in. of boiling water in a saucepan. Cover and steam for 5-8 minutes or until crisp-tender. Rinse in cold water; drain well. In a bowl, combine broccoli, cheese, ham, onions, parsley, nutmeg, salt and pepper.

On a floured surface, roll out pastry; cut each in half. Place 1-1/2 cups filling on one side of each half; flatten filling with a spoon. Combine egg and cream; brush some over pastry edges. Fold pastry over filling. Seal edges and prick tops with a fork.

Place on a baking sheet; brush with remaining egg

mixture. Bake at 400° for 18-22 minutes or until golden brown. Let stand 5 minutes before serving. **Yield:** 4 servings.

Ham 'n' Egg Sandwich

DeeDee Newton, Toronto, Ontario

This all-in-one breakfast is one of my most-requested recipes. I stack deli ham, tomato, scrambled eggs, onion and cheddar cheese inside a loaf of French bread, wrap it in foil and then warm it in the oven.

    1 unsliced loaf (1 pound) French bread
    4 tablespoons butter, softened, *divided*
    2 tablespoons mayonnaise
    8 thin slices deli ham
    1 large tomato, sliced
    1 small onion, thinly sliced
    8 eggs, lightly beaten
    8 slices cheddar cheese

Cut bread in half lengthwise; carefully hollow out top and bottom, leaving 1/2-in. shells (discard removed bread or save for another use). Spread 3 tablespoons of butter and all of the mayonnaise inside bread shells. Line bottom bread shell with ham; top with tomato and onion.

In a skillet, melt remaining butter; add eggs. Cook over medium heat, stirring occasionally until edges are almost set. Spoon into bottom bread shell; top with cheese. Cover with bread top. Wrap in greased foil. Bake at 375° for 15-20 minutes or until heated through. Cut into serving-size pieces. **Yield:** 6-8 servings.

Ham 'n' Egg Sandwich

Curried Crab Quiche (p. 75)

Chapter 5

Holiday Favorites

From Christmas Day to Easter Sunday, special occasions are extra memorable with these seasonal and festive breakfasts.

Lemon Curd Coffee Cake

Lemon Curd Coffee Cake

Anne Wickman, Endicott, New York

I tried this recipe for my son's birthday and fell in love with the tart lemon filling. A confectioners'-sugar glaze and coconut topping make the coffee cake impressive for a brunch or afternoon gathering.

  1/2 cup all-purpose flour
  1/3 cup sugar
    3 tablespoons cold butter
  1/2 cup flaked coconut
BATTER:
 2-1/4 cups all-purpose flour
  1/2 teaspoon salt
  1/2 teaspoon baking powder
  1/2 teaspoon baking soda
  3/4 cup cold butter
  2/3 cup vanilla yogurt
    1 tablespoon lemon juice
    2 teaspoons grated lemon peel
    1 egg
    1 egg yolk
  1/2 cup lemon curd
GLAZE:
  1/2 cup confectioners' sugar
    1 teaspoon water
    1 teaspoon lemon juice

In a small bowl, combine the flour and sugar. Cut in butter until mixture resembles coarse crumbs. Stir in coconut; set aside.

For the batter, in a large bowl, combine the flour, salt, baking powder and baking soda. Cut in the butter until the mixture resembles coarse crumbs. Combine the vanilla yogurt, lemon juice, lemon peel, egg and egg yolk; stir into the crumb mixture just until moistened (batter will be stiff).

Spread 2 cups batter in a greased 9-in. springform pan; sprinkle with 3/4 cup of the coconut crumb mixture. Drop 1/2 teaspoonfuls of lemon curd over the top to within 1/2 in. of the edge. Carefully spoon the remaining batter over lemon curd; sprinkle with the remaining coconut mixture.

Place pan on a baking sheet. Bake at 350° for 55-60 minutes or until a toothpick comes out clean. Cool for 10 minutes. Carefully run a knife around the edge of pan to loosen; remove sides of pan. Combine the glaze ingredients; drizzle over warm cake. **Yield:** 12 servings.

Golden Shrimp Brunch Casserole

Marilyn Bagshaw, San Rafael, California

During the 1940s, my mother got together with a close group of friends regularly for lunch. This was one of Mom's favorite recipes to share.

    6 eggs
 2-1/2 cups milk
    2 tablespoons minced fresh parsley
  3/4 teaspoon ground mustard
  1/2 teaspoon salt
   10 slices bread, crusts removed and cubed
    2 cups frozen cooked salad shrimp, thawed
    1 block (8 ounces) process cheese (Velveeta),
      cut into thin strips

In a large bowl, whisk the eggs, milk, parsley, mustard and salt. In a greased 11-in. x 7-in. x 2-in. baking dish, layer bread cubes, shrimp and cheese; pour egg mixture over top.

Bake, uncovered, at 325° for 50-55 minutes or until mixture is set and top is puffed and golden. Let stand for 10 minutes before serving. **Yield:** 6 servings.

Golden Shrimp Brunch Casserole

Pumpkin Pancakes

Brenda Parker, Portage, Michigan

The flavors of fall star in these light, fluffy pancakes. Not only do they have pumpkin and cinnamon in the batter, they're served with a homemade apple syrup. I enjoy these goodies so much that I'll even eat them as a snack.

HOT CIDER SYRUP:
- 3/4 cup apple cider *or* juice
- 1/2 cup packed brown sugar
- 1/2 cup corn syrup
- 2 tablespoons butter
- 1/2 teaspoon lemon juice
- 1/8 teaspoon ground cinnamon
- 1/8 teaspoon ground nutmeg

PANCAKES:
- 1 cup all-purpose flour
- 1 tablespoon sugar
- 2 teaspoons baking powder
- 1/2 teaspoon salt
- 1/2 teaspoon ground cinnamon
- 2 eggs, *separated*
- 1 cup milk
- 1/2 cup canned pumpkin
- 2 tablespoons vegetable oil

In a saucepan, combine the syrup ingredients. Bring to a boil over medium heat, stirring occasionally. Reduce heat; simmer, uncovered, for 20-25 minutes or until slightly thickened. Let stand for 30 minutes before serving.

For pancakes, combine the flour, sugar, baking powder, salt and cinnamon in a bowl. In another bowl, whisk the egg yolks, milk, pumpkin and oil. Stir into the dry ingredients just until moistened. In a mixing bowl, beat the egg whites until soft peaks form; fold into pancake batter.

Pour batter by 1/4 cupfuls onto a hot greased griddle. Turn when bubbles form on top of pancakes. Cook until second side is golden brown. Serve with the syrup. **Yield:** 15 pancakes (1 cup syrup).

Sunday Brunch Eggs

Judy Wells, Phoenix, Arizona

Nestled on top of Canadian bacon and Swiss cheese, these crowd-pleasing eggs are drizzled with rich cream, sprinkled with Parmesan and baked in the oven. For a pretty presentation, cut around each egg and serve it on toast.

- 12 slices Canadian bacon
- 12 slices Swiss cheese
- 12 eggs
- 1 cup heavy whipping cream
- 1/3 cup grated Parmesan cheese
- 12 slices toast, optional

French Toast Easter Eggs

Place Canadian bacon in a greased 13-in. x 9-in. x 2-in. baking dish; top with Swiss cheese. Carefully break an egg over each piece of cheese. Pour cream over eggs and sprinkle with Parmesan cheese.

Bake, uncovered, at 375° for 20-25 minutes or until eggs reach desired doneness. Let stand for 5 minutes. Cut between each egg; serve on toast if desired. **Yield:** 6 servings.

French Toast Easter Eggs

Here's a festive Easter treat and easy brunch dish—all rolled into one! Our Test Kitchen staff cut the bread with an egg-shaped cookie cutter, prepared it the same as traditional French toast and "dyed" the pieces with jellies.

- 1 loaf (1 pound) French bread, cut into 3/4-inch slices
- 4 eggs
- 2/3 cup orange juice
- 2 tablespoons sugar
- 1 teaspoon grated orange peel
- 1/4 teaspoon salt
- 1/4 cup butter

Strawberry, mint and grape jellies

Cut each slice of bread with a 3-in. oval cookie cutter to create Easter egg shapes; discard crust. In a bowl, beat eggs, orange juice, sugar, orange peel and salt. Melt butter in a large skillet. Dip both sides of bread into egg mixture; cook in butter until golden brown on both sides.

Meanwhile, heat jellies in separate microwave-safe bowls just until warm. Transfer each to a separate plastic or pastry bag; cut a small hole in the corner of bag. Decorate French toast in a striped pattern or as desired to resemble Easter eggs. **Yield:** 6-8 servings.

Home-for-Christmas Fruit Bake

Home-for-Christmas Fruit Bake

Bonnie Baumgardner, Sylva, North Carolina

When the cinnamon aroma of this dish fills the house, mouths start to water in anticipation! The fruit comes out tender and slightly tart while the pecans add a pleasing crunch.

- 1 medium apple, peeled and thinly sliced
- 1 teaspoon lemon juice
- 1 can (20 ounces) pineapple chunks
- 1 can (29 ounces) peach halves, drained
- 1 can (29 ounces) pear halves, drained
- 1 jar (6 ounces) maraschino cherries, drained
- 1/2 cup pecan halves
- 1/3 cup packed brown sugar
- 1 tablespoon butter
- 1 teaspoon ground cinnamon

Toss apple slices with lemon juice. Arrange in a greased 2-1/2-qt. baking dish. Drain pineapple, reserving 1/4 cup juice. Combine pineapple, peaches and pears; spoon over apples. Top with cherries and pecans; set aside.

In a small saucepan, combine brown sugar, butter, cinnamon and reserved pineapple juice. Cook and stir over low heat until sugar is dissolved and butter is melted. Pour over fruit. Bake, uncovered, at 325° for 45 minutes or until apples are tender. Serve warm. **Yield: 12-14 servings.**

Bacon Roll-Ups

Janet Abate, North Brunswick, New Jersey

This favorite family recipe dates back to the 1930s, when my grandmother made these hearty rolls for breakfast.

- 1/3 cup finely chopped onion
- 1 tablespoon butter
- 3 cups cubed day-old bread
- 1/4 teaspoon celery salt
- 1/4 teaspoon garlic powder
- 1/8 teaspoon salt
- 1/8 teaspoon pepper
- 1 egg, lightly beaten
- 10 bacon strips

In a small skillet, saute onion in butter until tender. In a bowl, combine the bread cubes, celery salt, garlic powder, salt, pepper and onion mixture; toss to mix evenly. Add egg; toss to coat bread cubes. Roll into ten 1-1/4-in. balls. Wrap a bacon strip around each ball. Secure with a toothpick. Repeat with remaining ingredients.

In a large skillet, cook bacon roll-ups on all sides over medium heat for 18 minutes or until bacon is crisp and a meat thermometer inserted into stuffing reads at least 160°. Drain on paper towels. **Yield: 10 roll-ups.**

Onion Potato Pie

Gwyn Frasco, Walla Walla, Washington

I jazzed up a basic hash-brown bake by tossing in plenty of sweet onions, for which our area is famous.

- 8 cups frozen shredded hash brown potatoes, thawed
- 6 tablespoons butter, *divided*
- 3/4 teaspoon salt, *divided*
- 1 cup diced sweet onion
- 1/4 cup chopped sweet red pepper
- 1 cup (4 ounces) shredded cheddar cheese

3 eggs, lightly beaten
1/3 cup milk

Gently squeeze potatoes to remove excess water. Melt 5 tablespoons butter; add to potatoes along with 1/2 teaspoon salt. Press in bottom and up sides of a greased 9-in. pie plate to form a crust. Bake at 425° for 25-30 minutes or until edges are browned. Cool to room temperature.

In a saucepan over medium heat, saute the onion and red pepper in remaining butter until tender, about 6-8 minutes. Spoon into crust; sprinkle with cheese. Combine the eggs, milk and remaining salt; pour over onion mixture.

Bake at 350° for 20-25 minutes or until a knife inserted near the center comes out clean. Let stand 5 minutes before serving. **Yield:** 6-8 servings.

Canadian Bacon with Apples

Paula Marchesi, Lenhartsville, Pennsylvania

During the busy holiday season, I rely on this no-fuss recipe. A brown-sugar glaze and colorful apple wedges easily dress up the slices of Canadian bacon.

1/2 cup packed brown sugar
1 tablespoon lemon juice
1/8 teaspoon pepper
1 large unpeeled red apple
1 large unpeeled green apple
1 pound sliced Canadian bacon

In a large skillet, combine the brown sugar, lemon juice and pepper; mix well. Cook and stir over medium heat until the brown sugar is dissolved. Cut each apple into 16 wedges; add to the sugar mixture. Cook over medium heat for 5-7 minutes until tender, stirring occasionally. Remove the apples to a serving platter with a slotted spoon; keep warm.

Add Canadian bacon to the skillet; cook over medi-

Canadian Bacon with Apples

um heat for 3 minutes or until heated through, turning once. Transfer to platter. Pour remaining brown sugar mixture over apples and bacon. Serve immediately. **Yield:** 6 servings.

Gingerbread Waffles

At Christmastime, you don't have to confine the flavor of gingerbread to cookies! Spice up breakfast as well with these seasonally pleasing waffles. For an elegant touch, our Test Kitchen staff sprinkled them with confectioners' sugar.

1 cup all-purpose flour
1-1/2 teaspoons baking powder
1 teaspoon ground ginger
3/4 teaspoon ground cinnamon
1/2 teaspoon baking soda
1/4 teaspoon salt
1/8 teaspoon ground cloves
1/3 cup packed brown sugar
1 egg, *separated*
3/4 cup buttermilk
1/4 cup molasses
3 tablespoons butter, melted
1/8 teaspoon cream of tartar
Confectioners' sugar, optional

In a large bowl, combine the first seven ingredients. In a small mixing bowl, beat the brown sugar and egg yolk until fluffy; add the buttermilk, molasses and butter. Stir into dry ingredients just until combined.

In a small mixing bowl, beat the egg white and cream of tartar until stiff peaks form. Gently fold into batter. Quickly spoon onto a preheated waffle iron. Bake according to manufacturer's directions until golden brown. Sprinkle with confectioners' sugar if desired. **Yield:** 8 waffles.

Cranberry Brunch Punch

Edie DeSpain, Logan, Utah

From Thanksgiving to New Year's Day and beyond, you can't miss when you offer this tangy punch. It's excellent poured over ice or served warm. For a fun garnish, thread fresh cranberries and orange slices on stir sticks.

4 cups cranberry juice
2 cups orange juice
1 cup pineapple juice
1/2 cup lemon juice
1/2 cup water
1/3 cup sugar
1 teaspoon almond extract

In a large container, combine ingredients; stir until sugar is dissolved. Refrigerate until serving. **Yield:** 2 quarts.

Stuffed French Toast

Stuffed French Toast

Edna Hoffman, Hebron, Indiana

I create pockets in thick French bread and stuff them with Swiss cheese and sizzling sausage patties. Just add maple syrup, and you've got a breakfast that can't be beat!

    8 slices French bread (1-1/2 inches thick)
    2 tablespoons butter, softened
    1 package (8 ounces) brown-and-serve
      sausage patties, cooked
    1 cup (4 ounces) shredded Swiss cheese
    2 eggs
  1/2 cup milk
1-1/2 teaspoons sugar
  1/4 teaspoon ground cinnamon
Maple syrup, optional

Cut a pocket in the crust of each slice of bread. Butter the inside of pocket. Cut sausage into bite-size pieces; toss with cheese. Stuff into pockets.

   In a shallow bowl, beat eggs, milk, sugar and cinnamon; dip both sides of bread. Cook on a greased hot griddle until golden brown on both sides. Serve with syrup if desired. **Yield: 4 servings.**

Eggnog Pancakes with Cranberry Sauce

Iola Egle, Bella Vista, Arkansas

It's not difficult to dress up ordinary pancakes for the holiday season—this recipe proves it! We love the subtle eggnog flavor and tangy cranberry sauce as a topping.

    2 cups pancake mix
    1 egg
1-1/2 cups eggnog
1-1/2 teaspoons vanilla extract
Pinch ground nutmeg
    1 can (16 ounces) whole-berry *or* jellied
      cranberry sauce

Place pancake mix in a bowl. In another bowl, whisk egg, eggnog, vanilla and nutmeg; stir into pancake mix just until moistened.

   Pour batter by 1/3 cupfuls onto a lightly greased hot griddle; turn when bubbles form on top of pancakes. Cook until second side is golden brown. Serve with cranberry sauce. **Yield: 6 servings (12 pancakes).**

Easter Brunch Lasagna

Sarah Larson, La Farge, Wisconsin

Ham, broccoli and hard-cooked eggs are terrific together in this unique lasagna. I made it for a family gathering and rounded out the menu with fresh fruit and muffins.

  1/2 cup butter
  1/3 cup all-purpose flour
  1/4 teaspoon salt
Dash white pepper
    3 cups milk
  1/4 cup finely chopped green onions
    1 teaspoon lemon juice
  1/4 teaspoon hot pepper sauce
    9 lasagna noodles, cooked and drained
    2 cups diced fully cooked ham
    1 package (10 ounces) frozen chopped
      broccoli, thawed
  1/2 cup grated Parmesan cheese

Easter Brunch Lasagna

3 cups (12 ounces) shredded cheddar cheese
4 hard-cooked eggs, finely chopped

In a heavy saucepan, melt butter over medium heat. Stir in flour, salt and pepper until smooth. Gradually add milk. Bring to a boil; cook and stir for 2 minutes or until thickened. Remove from the heat; stir in the onions, lemon juice and hot pepper sauce.

Spread a fourth of the white sauce in a greased 13-in. x 9-in. x 2-in. baking dish. Layer with three noodles, half of the ham and broccoli, 3 tablespoons Parmesan cheese, 1 cup cheddar cheese, half of the eggs and a fourth of the white sauce. Repeat layers. Top with the remaining noodles, white sauce and cheeses.

Bake, uncovered, at 350° for 40-45 minutes or until bubbly. Let stand for 15 minutes before cutting. **Yield:** 12 servings.

Traditional Hot Cross Buns

Chocolate-Cherry Cream Crepes

Kimberly Witt, Minot, North Dakota

My son calls me a gourmet cook whenever I fix these fancy, golden crepes. Sometimes I replace the cherry pie filling with apple and drizzle the crepes with warm caramel sauce.

1-1/4 cups milk
    3 eggs
    2 tablespoons butter, melted
  3/4 cup all-purpose flour
    1 tablespoon sugar
  1/4 teaspoon salt
    1 package (8 ounces) cream cheese, softened
  1/2 cup confectioners' sugar
    1 teaspoon vanilla extract
    1 can (21 ounces) cherry pie filling
Chocolate fudge ice cream topping and whipped topping

In a large mixing bowl, combine the milk, eggs and butter. Combine the flour, sugar and salt; add to egg mixture. Cover and refrigerate for 1 hour. For filling, in a small mixing bowl, beat cream cheese until smooth. Beat in confectioners' sugar and vanilla until smooth; set aside.

Heat a lightly greased 8-in. nonstick skillet; pour 2 tablespoons batter into the center of skillet. Lift and tilt pan to evenly coat bottom. Cook until top appears dry; turn and cook 15-20 seconds longer. Remove to a wire rack. Repeat with remaining batter, greasing skillet as needed. Stack crepes with waxed paper between. Cover and freeze 10 crepes for another use. Crepes may be frozen for up to 3 months.

Pipe filling onto the center of each remaining crepe. Top with 2 tablespoons pie filling. Fold side edges of crepe to the center. Drizzle with fudge topping and garnish with whipped topping. Serve immediately. **Yield:** 8 servings.

Traditional Hot Cross Buns

Barbara Jean Lull, Fullerton, California

Topped with a white glaze in the shape of a cross, these yeast rolls dotted with raisins and currants are old-fashioned Easter favorites.

    2 packages (1/4 ounce *each*) active dry yeast
    2 cups warm milk (110° to 115°)
  1/3 cup butter, softened
    2 eggs, lightly beaten
  1/4 cup sugar
1-1/2 teaspoons salt
    6 to 7 cups all-purpose flour
  1/2 cup raisins
  1/2 cup dried currants
    1 teaspoon ground cinnamon
  1/4 teaspoon ground allspice
    2 tablespoons water
    1 egg yolk
Confectioners' sugar icing

In a mixing bowl, dissolve yeast in milk. Stir in butter, eggs, sugar and salt. Combine 3 cups flour, raisins, currants, cinnamon and allspice; add to yeast mixture and mix well. Stir in enough remaining flour to form a soft dough.

Turn onto a floured surface and knead until smooth and elastic, about 6-8 minutes. Place in a greased bowl, turning once to grease top. Cover and let rise in a warm place until doubled, about 1 hour.

Punch dough down; shape into 1-1/2- to 2-in. balls. Place 2 in. apart on greased baking sheets. Using a sharp knife, cut a cross on top of each roll. Cover and let rise until doubled, about 30 minutes.

Beat the water and egg yolk; brush over the rolls. Bake at 375° for 15-20 minutes or until golden brown. Cool on wire racks. Pipe confectioners' sugar icing over the rolls. **Yield:** 2-1/2 dozen.

Jolly Jelly Doughnuts

Lee Bremson, Kansas City, Missouri

Just looking at these plump jelly-filled doughnuts makes your mouth water! Serve them warm, and folks will be licking sugar from their fingers and asking for seconds.

> 2 packages (1/4 ounce *each*) active dry yeast
> 2 cups warm milk (110° to 115°)
> 7 cups all-purpose flour, *divided*
> 4 egg yolks
> 1 egg
> 1/2 cup sugar
> 1 teaspoon salt
> 2 teaspoons grated lemon peel
> 1/2 teaspoon vanilla extract
> 1/2 cup butter, melted

Oil for deep-fat frying
Red jelly of your choice
Additional sugar

In a large mixing bowl, dissolve yeast in warm milk. Add 2 cups flour; mix well. Let stand in a warm place for 30 minutes. Add the egg yolks, egg, sugar, salt, lemon peel and vanilla; mix well. Beat in butter and remaining flour. Do not knead. Cover and let rise in a warm place until doubled, about 45 minutes.

Punch dough down. On a lightly floured surface, roll out to 1/2 in. thickness. Cut with a 2-1/2-in. biscuit cutter. Place on lightly greased baking sheets. Cover and let rise until nearly double, about 35 minutes.

In a deep-fat fryer or electric skillet, heat oil to 375°. Fry doughnuts, a few at a time, for 1-1/2 to 2 minutes on each side or until browned. Drain on paper towels. Cool for 2-3 minutes; cut a small slit with a sharp knife on one side of each doughnut. Using a pastry bag with a small round tip or a small spoon, fill each doughnut with about 1 teaspoon jelly. Carefully roll doughnuts in sugar. Serve warm. **Yield:** about 2-1/2 dozen.

Jolly Jelly Doughnuts

Cherry Chip Scones

Cherry Chip Scones

Pamela Brooks, South Berwick, Maine

Dotted with dried cherries and vanilla chips, these buttery scones are so sweet and flaky that I sometimes make them for dessert. They're wonderful with your favorite tea.

> 3 cups all-purpose flour
> 1/2 cup sugar
> 2-1/2 teaspoons baking powder
> 1/2 teaspoon baking soda
> 6 tablespoons cold butter
> 1 cup (8 ounces) vanilla yogurt
> 1/4 cup plus 2 tablespoons milk, *divided*
> 1-1/3 cups dried cherries
> 2/3 cup vanilla *or* white chips

In a large bowl, combine the flour, sugar, baking powder and baking soda. Cut in butter until the mixture resembles coarse crumbs. Combine yogurt and 1/4 cup milk; stir into crumb mixture just until moistened. Knead in the cherries and chips.

On a greased baking sheet, pat the dough into a 9-in. circle. Cut into eight wedges; separate wedges. Brush with the remaining milk. Bake at 400° for 20-25 minutes or until golden brown. Serve warm. **Yield:** 8 servings.

Taste Twist

Feel free to vary the ingredients a bit in Cherry Chip Scones (on this page). Try dried cranberries instead of cherries...or replace the vanilla chips with chocolate.

Sweetheart Pancakes

Surprise that special someone with this lovely breakfast on Valentine's Day or anytime. Our Test Kitchen staff topped these hot-off-the-griddle goodies with whipped cream and a luscious cherry sauce.

- 1-3/4 cups all-purpose flour
- 2 tablespoons sugar
- 2 teaspoons baking powder
- 1/2 teaspoon salt
- 2 eggs
- 1-1/2 cups milk
- 3 tablespoons vegetable oil
- 1/2 teaspoon lemon juice

CHERRY SAUCE:
- 1 can (21 ounces) cherry pie filling
- 1/2 to 3/4 teaspoon almond extract
- 1/8 to 1/4 teaspoon ground nutmeg

Whipped cream in a can

In a bowl, combine the flour, sugar, baking powder and salt. In another bowl, beat the eggs; add milk, oil and lemon juice. Stir into dry ingredients just until moistened.

Pour batter by 1/3 cupfuls onto a lightly greased hot griddle; turn when bubbles form on top of pancakes. Cook until the second side is golden brown.

For cherry sauce, combine pie filling, extract and nutmeg in a medium saucepan. Cook, stirring occasionally, until heated through.

To serve as shown in the photo, stack pancakes on serving plates and make a heart outline with whipped cream; spoon cherry sauce into heart. **Yield:** 4 servings (12 pancakes).

Artichoke Cheese Oven Omelet

Bonnie Hawkins, Burlington, Wisconsin

My husband likes to cook, and everyone enjoys his cheesy artichoke omelet. It looks impressive garnished with chopped tomatoes, ripe olives and chives.

- 3/4 cup salsa
- 1 can (14 ounces) water-packed artichoke hearts, rinsed, drained and chopped
- 1 cup (4 ounces) shredded Monterey Jack cheese
- 1 cup (4 ounces) shredded cheddar cheese
- 1/4 cup grated Parmesan cheese
- 6 eggs, beaten
- 1 cup (8 ounces) sour cream

Chopped fresh tomatoes, sliced ripe olives and minced chives, optional

Spread salsa in a greased 9-in. deep-dish pie plate. Top with the artichoke hearts and cheese. In a bowl, whisk the eggs and sour cream. Pour over the cheeses.

Bake, uncovered, at 350° for 25-30 minutes or until a knife inserted near the center comes out clean. Let stand for 5 minutes before cutting. Garnish with tomatoes, olives and chives if desired. **Yield:** 6-8 servings.

Sweetheart Pancakes

Cranberry-Apple Biscuits

Cranberry-Apple Biscuits

A tangy cranberry-apple topping and tender biscuits blend beautifully in this pretty treat from our Test Kitchen home economists. It could even make a unique dessert served with vanilla ice cream.

    2 tablespoons butter, melted
    2 tablespoons sugar
    1/4 teaspoon ground cinnamon
    1/4 teaspoon ground ginger
    1 tube (17.3 ounces) large refrigerated
        biscuits
SAUCE:
    3/4 cup sugar
    1/2 teaspoon ground cinnamon
    1/2 teaspoon ground ginger
    3 cups diced peeled tart apples
    1 cup fresh *or* frozen cranberries
    1/2 cup water, *divided*
    1 tablespoon lemon juice
    2 tablespoons cornstarch

Place butter in a shallow bowl. In another shallow bowl, combine the sugar, cinnamon and ginger. Dip the top of each biscuit in butter, then in sugar mixture. Place sugar side up 2 in. apart on an ungreased baking sheet. Bake at 350° for 15-17 minutes or until golden brown. Remove to a wire rack.

For sauce, in a saucepan, combine the sugar, cinnamon and ginger. Add the apples, cranberries, 1/4 cup water and lemon juice. Bring to a boil. Reduce heat; cover and simmer for 3-4 minutes, stirring occasionally. Combine cornstarch and remaining water until smooth. Stir into fruit mixture. Bring to a boil; cook and stir for 2 minutes or until thickened. Pour about 1/3 cup sauce over each biscuit. **Yield:** 8 servings.

Pecan-Stuffed Waffles

Jenny Flake, Gilbert, Arizona

This recipe is perfect for entertaining because it's impressive yet extremely simple to prepare. The creamy brown sugar and pecan filling between the waffles is delectable!

    8 frozen waffles
    2 packages (3 ounces *each*) cream cheese,
        softened
    1/2 cup packed brown sugar
    1-1/2 teaspoons ground cinnamon
    1 teaspoon vanilla extract
    1/2 cup chopped pecans
    1 cup maple syrup
Confectioners' sugar
    4 fresh strawberries, cut in half

Toast waffles according to package directions. In a small mixing bowl, beat the cream cheese, brown sugar, cinnamon and vanilla until smooth. Stir in pecans. Spread over four waffles; top with remaining waffles. Drizzle with syrup. Sprinkle with confectioners' sugar; garnish with a strawberry. **Yield:** 4 servings.

Frosty Mocha Drink

Lauren Nance, San Diego, California

I whip up this chocolaty drink when friends drop in. For a richer version, replace the milk with half-and-half cream.

    1 cup milk
    3 tablespoons instant chocolate drink mix
    2 tablespoons instant coffee granules

Frosty Mocha Drink

2 tablespoons honey
1 teaspoon vanilla extract
14 to 16 ice cubes

In a blender, combine all ingredients; cover and process until smooth. Pour into chilled glasses; serve immediately. **Yield:** 4 servings.

Sweet Potato Muffins

Susan Bracken, State College, Pennsylvania

Ginger really enhances the flavor of these yummy muffins and the accompanying butter. They're best served warm.

1-1/2 cups all-purpose flour
   1 cup plus 1 tablespoon sugar, *divided*
   3 teaspoons baking powder
   3 teaspoons grated orange peel
1-1/2 teaspoons ground ginger
   1 teaspoon baking soda
  1/4 teaspoon salt
   2 eggs, lightly beaten
   1 cup cold mashed sweet potatoes (prepared without milk or butter)
  1/4 teaspoon ground cinnamon
GINGER BUTTER:
  1/2 cup butter, softened
   2 tablespoons finely chopped crystallized ginger

In a large bowl, combine the flour, 1 cup sugar, baking powder, orange peel, ginger, baking soda and salt. Combine eggs and sweet potatoes; stir into dry ingredients just until moistened.

Fill greased or paper-lined muffin cups two-thirds full. Combine cinnamon and remaining sugar; sprinkle over batter. Bake at 400° for 18-22 minutes or until a toothpick comes out clean. Cool for 5 minutes before removing from pans to wire racks. In a small bowl, combine the ginger butter ingredients. Serve with warm muffins. **Yield:** 1 dozen.

No-Turn Omelet

Helen Clem, Creston, Iowa

With sausage, eggs, cheese and peppers, this oven-baked dish tastes like a strata. It's so delicious and easy to fix, it just might become your favorite omelet!

   8 eggs, beaten
   2 cups cooked crumbled sausage *or* cubed fully cooked ham
   2 cups cubed process cheese (Velveeta)
   2 cups milk
   1 cup crushed saltines (about 24 crackers)
  1/4 cup chopped onion
  1/4 cup chopped green pepper

Pumpkin Doughnut Drops

  1/4 cup chopped sweet red pepper
  1/2 to 1 teaspoon salt

Combine all ingredients in a large bowl; pour into a greased shallow 3-qt. or 12-in. x 9-in. x 2-in. baking dish. Bake, uncovered, at 350° for 45 minutes or until a knife inserted near the center comes out clean. Let stand for 5 minutes before serving. **Yield:** 8-10 servings.

Pumpkin Doughnut Drops

Beva Staum, Muscoda, Wisconsin

I always like to have some special goodies on hand when my grandchildren visit. Their eyes light up when they see these sugarcoated doughnut bites.

   2 eggs
1-1/4 cups sugar
   2 tablespoons shortening
   1 cup canned pumpkin
   2 teaspoons white vinegar
   1 teaspoon vanilla extract
   3 cups all-purpose flour
  1/2 cup nonfat dry milk powder
   3 teaspoons baking powder
  1/2 teaspoon salt
  1/2 teaspoon ground cinnamon
  1/2 teaspoon ground nutmeg
  1/2 cup lemon-lime soda
Oil for deep-fat frying
Additional sugar

In a mixing bowl, beat the eggs, sugar and shortening. Add the pumpkin, vinegar and vanilla. Combine the dry ingredients; add to the pumpkin mixture alternately with soda.

In an electric skillet or deep-fat fryer, heat oil to 375°. Drop teaspoonfuls of batter, a few at a time, into hot oil. Fry for 1 minute on each side or until golden brown. Drain on paper towels; roll in sugar while warm. **Yield:** about 7 dozen.

Frozen Fruit Cups

Frozen Fruit Cups

Patricia Throlson, Hawick, Minnesota

This colorful medley is so refreshing and pretty for special occasions. You can either freeze the fruit mixture in disposable, clear plastic glasses or use cupcake liners placed in sauce dishes or sherbet glasses.

✓ **Uses less fat, sugar or salt. Includes Nutrition Facts and Diabetic Exchanges.**

- 2 cans (20 ounces *each*) crushed pineapple, undrained
- 2 packages (10 ounces *each*) frozen sweetened strawberries, thawed
- 1 can (20 ounces) fruit cocktail, undrained
- 1 can (12 ounces) frozen orange juice concentrate, thawed
- 1 can (6 ounces) frozen lemonade concentrate, thawed
- 6 medium firm bananas, cubed

In a large bowl, combine all ingredients. Pour into foil-lined muffin cups or individual plastic beverage glasses. Freeze until solid. When ready to serve, thaw for 30-45 minutes before serving. **Yield:** 10 servings.

Nutrition Facts: One 3/4-cup serving (prepared with unsweetened pineapple and fruit cocktail in light syrup) equals 259 calories, 1 g fat (0 saturated fat), 0 cholesterol, 7 mg sodium, 64 g carbohydrate, 0 fiber, 3 g protein. **Diabetic Exchange:** 4 fruit.

Valentine Coffee Cake

Dolores Skrout, Summerhill, Pennsylvania

Your loved ones are sure to appreciate this heart-shaped coffee cake. It's perfect for a bridal shower or tea party, too.

- 4-1/2 to 5 cups all-purpose flour, *divided*
- 1/2 cup sugar
- 1-1/2 teaspoons salt
- 2 packages (1/4 ounce *each*) active dry yeast
- 1/2 cup milk
- 1/2 cup water
- 6 tablespoons butter, *divided*
- 2 eggs

FILLING:
- 3/4 cup packed dark brown sugar
- 1/2 cup chopped blanched almonds, toasted
- 1/3 cup chopped maraschino cherries
- 1 tablespoon all-purpose flour
- 2 teaspoons almond extract

GLAZE:
- 1-1/2 cups confectioners' sugar
- 2 tablespoons butter, softened
- 2 to 3 tablespoons milk
- 1/2 teaspoon vanilla extract

In a mixing bowl, combine 1-1/2 cups flour, sugar, salt and yeast. Heat milk, water and 4 tablespoons butter to 120°-130°. Gradually add to dry ingredients; beat on medium for 2 minutes. Add eggs and 1/2 cup flour; beat on high for 2 minutes. By hand, add enough remaining flour to form a soft dough.

Turn onto a floured surface; knead until smooth and elastic, about 6-8 minutes. Place in a greased bowl, turning once to grease top. Cover and let rise in a warm place until doubled, about 1 hour.

Punch dough down. Divide in half. Roll each half into a 26-in. x 8-in. rectangle. Melt remaining butter; brush over dough. Combine filling ingredients; sprinkle over butter. Roll up jelly-roll style from long end; pinch to seal. Place seam side down on greased nonstick baking sheets or baking sheets lined with parchment paper. Shape each roll into heart; seal ends. Cut from outer edge two-thirds through cake every 1 in. and turn each section out. Cover and let rise until doubled, about 1 hour.

Bake at 350° for 15-20 minutes or until golden. Remove immediately from baking sheets to wire racks. Cool completely; remove parchment paper if used. For glaze, cream sugar and butter. Stir in milk and vanilla until smooth. Drizzle over hearts. **Yield:** 2 coffee cakes.

Maple Hot Chocolate

Marla Brenneman, Goshen, Indiana

What sweet beverage is more popular in cold weather than hot chocolate? The subtle maple flavoring in this recipe puts a yummy spin on this family-favorite treat.

1/4 cup sugar
1 tablespoon baking cocoa
1/8 teaspoon salt
1/4 cup hot water
1 tablespoon butter
4 cups milk
12 large marshmallows, *divided*
1 teaspoon maple flavoring
1 teaspoon vanilla extract

In a large saucepan, combine sugar, cocoa and salt. Stir in water until smooth. Add butter; bring to a boil. Reduce heat. Add milk, eight marshmallows and flavorings; simmer until marshmallows are melted. Pour into mugs; top each with a marshmallow. **Yield:** 4 servings.

Apricot Cranberry Bread

Diane Roth, Milwaukee, Wisconsin

I was making cranberry bread one day when I found a jar of apricot jam in the fridge and spooned some into the batter. The end result was scrumptious!

2 cups all-purpose flour
1 cup sugar
1 to 2 teaspoons grated orange peel
1-1/2 teaspoons baking powder
1/2 teaspoon baking soda
1/2 teaspoon salt
1 egg
3/4 cup water
1/4 cup vegetable oil

Apricot Cranberry Bread

Sausage Pinwheels

1 cup fresh *or* frozen halved cranberries
1/4 cup apricot preserves

In a large bowl, combine flour, sugar, orange peel, baking powder, baking soda and salt. In a small bowl, beat egg, water and oil; stir into dry ingredients just until moistened. Fold in the cranberries.

Pour into a greased and floured 9-in. x 5-in. x 3-in. loaf pan. Cut apricots in the preserves into small pieces; spoon preserves over batter. Cut through batter with a knife to swirl. Bake at 350° for 65-70 minutes or until a toothpick inserted near the center comes out clean. Cool for 10 minutes; remove from pan to a wire rack. **Yield:** 1 loaf.

Sausage Pinwheels

Gail Sykora, Menomonee Falls, Wisconsin

These savory spirals make ordinary sausage impressive for holiday buffets. Our guests eagerly help themselves, and sometimes these eye-catching pinwheels never make it to their plates!

1 tube (8 ounces) refrigerated crescent rolls
1/2 pound uncooked bulk pork sausage
2 tablespoons minced chives

Unroll crescent roll dough on a lightly floured surface; press seams and perforations together. Roll into a 14-in. x 10-in. rectangle. Spread sausage to within 1/2 in. of edges. Sprinkle with chives. Carefully roll up from a long side; cut into 12 slices.

Place 1 in. apart in an ungreased 15-in. x 10-in. x 1-in. baking pan. Bake at 375° for 12-16 minutes or until golden brown. **Yield:** 1 dozen.

Bacon 'n' Egg Bundles

Bacon 'n' Egg Bundles

Edith Landinger, Longview, Texas

These delightfully different cups give you hearty bacon and eggs all in one bite. The four-ingredient recipe can easily be doubled for a larger group, too.

　　1　teaspoon butter
　12　to 18 bacon strips
　　6　eggs
Fresh parsley sprigs

Lightly grease six muffin cups with the butter. In a large skillet, cook the bacon over medium heat until cooked but not crisp. Drain on paper towels.

　Cut six bacon strips in half width-wise; line the bottom of each muffin cup with two bacon pieces. Line the sides of each muffin cup with one or two bacon strips. Break an egg into each cup.

　Bake, uncovered, at 325° for 12-18 minutes or until whites are completely set and yolks begin to thicken but are not firm. Transfer to a serving plate; surround with parsley. **Yield:** 6 servings.

Hot Ginger Coffee

Audrey Thibodeau, Lancaster, New Hampshire

On wintry days, this spiced drink really hits the spot and warms you up. It looks extra-special garnished with whipped cream, cinnamon sticks and orange peel.

　　6　tablespoons ground coffee (not instant)
　　1　tablespoon grated orange peel
　　1　tablespoon chopped crystallized *or* candied ginger
　1/2　teaspoon ground cinnamon
　　6　cups cold water
Whipped cream, cinnamon sticks *and/or* additional orange peel, optional

Combine the coffee, orange peel, ginger and cinnamon; pour into a coffee filter. Brew according to manufacturer's directions. Pour into mugs; garnish with whipped cream, cinnamon sticks and orange peel if desired. **Yield:** 6 servings.

　Editor's Note: Look for crystallized or candied ginger in the spice or baking section of your grocery store.

Twice-Baked Cheese Souffles

It's easy to impress guests when you serve these individual souffles from our Test Kitchen staff. You can partially bake and refrigerate them early in the morning, then add the remaining cheese and finish baking just before mealtime.

    3 tablespoons butter
1/4 cup all-purpose flour
    2 cups plus 2 tablespoons milk
1/4 teaspoon onion powder
1/4 teaspoon salt
1/8 teaspoon ground nutmeg
1/8 teaspoon pepper
    2 cups (8 ounces) shredded cheddar cheese, *divided*
    3 eggs, *separated*

In a saucepan, melt butter. Stir in flour until smooth. Gradually add milk, onion powder, salt, nutmeg and pepper. Bring to a boil; cook and stir for 2 minutes or until thickened. Reduce heat; add 1 cup cheese and stir until melted. Remove from the heat; set aside.

In a small mixing bowl, beat egg yolks until thick and lemon-colored, about 3 minutes. Stir in 1/3 cup hot cheese sauce. Return all to the pan; cook and stir for 1-2 minutes. Cool completely.

In another mixing bowl, beat egg whites on high speed until stiff peaks form. Gently fold into cooled cheese mixture. Pour into ungreased 1-cup souffle dishes or custard cups. Place in a shallow baking pan. Add 1 in. of hot water to pan. Bake, uncovered, at 325° for 20 minutes. Remove custard cups to wire racks to cool. Cover and refrigerate for up to 4 hours.

Remove from the refrigerator 30 minutes before baking. Uncover; sprinkle with remaining cheese. Bake at 425° for 15-20 minutes or until puffed and golden brown. **Yield:** 4 servings.

Curried Crab Quiche

(Pictured on page 60)

Kathy Kittell, Lenexa, Kansas

Curry and crab go together perfectly in this rich quiche. It tastes so good, no one guesses how simple it is to prepare.

    1 unbaked pastry shell (9 inches)
    6 to 8 ounces canned *or* frozen crabmeat, thawed, drained and cartilage removed
3/4 cup shredded Swiss cheese
    3 eggs
1-1/2 cups heavy whipping cream
1/2 to 1 teaspoon curry powder
1/2 teaspoon salt
Dash pepper

Line the unpricked pastry shell with a double thickness of heavy-duty foil. Bake at 450° for 5 minutes.

Remove the foil; bake 5 minutes longer. Remove shell from the oven; reduce heat to 375°. Sprinkle the crab and shredded Swiss cheese into shell.

In a bowl, beat the eggs. Add the heavy whipping cream, curry, salt and pepper; pour over the cheese. Cover the edges of the pastry with foil; bake for 30-35 minutes or until a knife inserted near the center comes out clean. **Yield:** 6-8 servings.

Citrus Tea Punch

Janet Maulick, White Haven, Pennsylvania

As soon as I see the first mint sprigs in my garden, I get out my signature recipe for punch. I've been making this for over 40 years, and my mother made it before I did.

    6 individual tea bags
    6 cups boiling water
1-1/2 cups sugar
    3 cups chilled club soda
    2 cups orange juice
    1 cup lemon juice
Crushed ice
Orange and lemon slices
Fresh mint sprigs, optional

Steep tea bags in boiling water for 15 minutes. Discard bags. Stir sugar into tea until dissolved.

Add the soda, orange juice and lemon juice; mix well. Refrigerate punch until chilled. Serve over ice. Garnish with orange and lemon slices and mint sprigs if desired. **Yield:** 3 quarts.

Citrus Tea Punch

Four-Fruit Smoothie (p. 82)
Orange Fruit Baskets (p. 83)
Honey Bear French Toast (p. 83)

Chapter 6
Kid-Pleasing Treats

Breakfast is child's play with the fun French toast, super smoothies, yummy fruit and other tops-for-tots food here.

Maple-Glazed Fruit Rings
Strawberry-Topped Waffles

Strawberry-Topped Waffles

Warm and chunky, this fruit sauce from our Test Kitchen staff takes just minutes to make. If you don't have cranberry juice, just substitute orange juice.

- 1 package (16 ounces) frozen unsweetened whole strawberries
- 1/2 cup cranberry juice, *divided*
- 2 tablespoons honey
- 2 tablespoons cornstarch
- 8 frozen waffles

In a saucepan, combine the strawberries, 1/4 cup cranberry juice and honey. Cook over low heat for 10 minutes, stirring occasionally.

In a small bowl, combine the cornstarch and remaining cranberry juice until smooth; stir into the strawberry mixture. Bring to a boil; cook and stir for 2 minutes or until thickened. Toast the waffles according to the package directions; top with the warm strawberry sauce. **Yield:** 4 servings.

Maple-Glazed Fruit Rings

These pineapple and orange slices from our home economists are sure to warm up everyone on winter mornings. You could also use the glaze to top ice cream or pound cake.

- 2 cans (8 ounces *each*) pineapple slices, drained
- 1 medium navel orange, peeled and sliced
- 1/4 cup maple syrup
- 2 tablespoons orange marmalade
- 1/4 teaspoon vanilla extract

Place pineapple and orange slices on a broiler pan. Combine the maple syrup, marmalade and vanilla; brush over fruit. Broil 4 in. from the heat for 4-5 minutes or until sauce is bubbly. Serve warm. **Yield:** 4 servings.

Chilled Fruit Cups

Andrea Hawthorne, Mozeman, Montana

Kids will happily eat fruit when they see these fun, frosty cups bursting with strawberries, sliced bananas and more. It's convenient to prepare these treats the day before and keep them in the freezer.

- 1 can (12 ounces) frozen pineapple juice concentrate, thawed
- 1 can (6 ounces) frozen orange juice concentrate, thawed
- 1 cup water
- 1 cup sugar
- 2 tablespoons lemon juice
- 3 medium firm bananas, sliced
- 1 package (16 ounces) frozen unsweetened strawberries
- 1 can (15 ounces) mandarin oranges, drained
- 1 can (8 ounces) crushed pineapple
- 18 clear plastic cups (9 ounces)

In a large bowl, prepare the pineapple juice concentrate according to package directions. Add the orange juice concentrate, water, sugar, lemon juice, bananas, berries, oranges and pineapple. Spoon 3/4 cupful into each plastic cup.

Place the fruit cups in a pan and freeze. Remove fruit cups from the freezer 40-50 minutes before serving. **Yield:** 18 servings.

Chilled Fruit Cups

Bacon Cheese Strips
Pizza Omelet

Bacon Cheese Strips

Linn Morrison, Mesilla Park, New Mexico

These topped toast slices are super for breakfast or as an appetizer. They've gone over big with both my family and my women's club.

   1/3 cup mayonnaise
     1 egg, beaten
   1/2 teaspoon Worcestershire sauce
   1/8 teaspoon ground mustard
     5 to 6 drops hot pepper sauce
Dash pepper
     1 cup (4 ounces) shredded cheddar cheese
     8 bacon strips, cooked and crumbled
     8 bread slices, crusts removed and toasted
Paprika, optional

In a bowl, combine the first seven ingredients; mix well. Stir in bacon. Spread over toast. Sprinkle with paprika if desired.

   Cut each slice of toast into three strips. Place on a baking sheet. Bake at 350° for 12-14 minutes or until cheese is melted. **Yield:** 2 dozen.

Pizza Omelet

Sandy Cork, Melvin, Michigan

For a kid-pleasing breakfast, you can't go wrong combining omelets with popular pizza. This cheesy creation with pepperoni and pizza sauce is always a hit in our house.

     2 eggs
     2 tablespoons milk
     1 tablespoon butter
   1/4 cup pizza sauce
   10 slices pepperoni
   1/4 cup shredded part-skim mozzarella cheese
     1 tablespoon shredded Parmesan cheese

In a bowl, beat the eggs and milk. In a skillet over medium heat, melt the butter. Add the egg mixture. As the eggs set, lift the edges, letting the uncooked portion flow underneath. When the eggs are completely set, remove from the heat.

   Spread pizza sauce over half of the eggs; top with pepperoni and mozzarella cheese. Fold omelet in half; sprinkle with Parmesan cheese. Serve immediately. **Yield:** 1 serving.

Orange Crunch Yogurt

It took mere minutes for our Test Kitchen staff to toss together these pretty parfaits. The crunchy granola and cashews contrast nicely with the mandarin oranges and yogurt.

- 1/3 cup granola cereal without raisins
- 1/3 cup flaked coconut
- 1/3 cup chopped cashews
- 4 cartons (6 ounces *each*) orange yogurt
- 1 can (11 ounces) mandarin oranges, drained

In a bowl, combine the granola, coconut and cashews. In each of four parfait glasses or bowls, layer half of a container of yogurt, 2 tablespoons granola mixture, 5 or 6 orange segments, remaining yogurt and remaining granola mixture. Garnish with remaining oranges. Serve immediately. **Yield:** 4 servings.

Smiley Face Pancakes

Janette Garner, Carmel, Indiana

It's easy to get kids going in the morning when their plates are stacked with these fun flapjacks. Children can even help stir up the batter.

- 2 cups biscuit/baking mix
- 1-1/4 cups milk
- 1 egg, beaten
- 2 tablespoons sugar
- 2 tablespoons lemon juice
- 1 teaspoon vanilla extract

Red, green, yellow and blue liquid *or* paste
food coloring
Maple syrup, optional

Orange Crunch Yogurt

In a bowl, combine the biscuit mix, milk, egg, sugar, lemon juice and vanilla; mix until smooth. Place 1 tablespoon of batter each in four bowls. Color one red, one green, one yellow and one blue. Drop remaining batter by 1/4 cupfuls onto a lightly greased hot griddle.

To create face, paint colored batter on pancakes with a new small paintbrush. Cook until bubbles form on the top. Turn and cook until second side is golden. Serve with syrup if desired. **Yield:** about 1 dozen.

Berry Banana Smoothies

Linda Barker, Mohawk, Michigan

My mom gave me the recipe for this thick and frothy drink sweetened with honey. I like these smoothies for breakfast and even as a snack before bedtime.

- 1-1/2 cups vanilla *or* plain yogurt
- 2/3 cup orange juice
- 2 medium ripe bananas, cut into chunks
- 1 cup halved fresh strawberries
- 2 teaspoons honey

In a blender, combine all ingredients; cover and process until smooth. Pour into chilled glasses; serve immediately. **Yield:** 2 servings.

Fluffy Scrambled Eggs

Terry Pfleghaar, Elk River, Minnesota

When our son is hungry for something other than cold cereal and milk, he often whips up these cheesy eggs. He's also made them while on camping trips.

Smiley Face Pancakes

6 eggs
1/4 cup evaporated milk *or* half-and-half cream
1/4 teaspoon salt
1/8 teaspoon pepper
1 tablespoon vegetable oil
2 tablespoons process cheese sauce

In a bowl, beat eggs, milk or cream, salt and pepper. In a skillet, heat oil; add egg mixture. Stir in cheese sauce. Cook and stir gently over medium heat until eggs are completely set. **Yield:** 3 servings.

Golden Smoothies

Nancy Schmidt, Delhi, California

These sunny sippers take no more effort to prepare than orange juice from concentrate. To make them extra-special, garnish glasses with orange slices and maraschino cherries.

✓ **Uses less fat, sugar or salt. Includes Nutrition Facts and Diabetic Exchanges.**

1-1/2 cups orange juice
1 carton (8 ounces) peach yogurt
1 can (5-1/2 ounces) apricot nectar
1 teaspoon honey
Orange slices and maraschino cherries, optional

Place the first four ingredients in a blender; cover and process until smooth. Pour into glasses; garnish with oranges and cherries if desired. **Yield:** 3 cups.

Nutrition Facts: One 3/4-cup serving (prepared with fat-free yogurt; calculated without fruit garnish) equals 128 calories, trace fat (0 saturated fat), 2 mg cholesterol, 37 mg sodium, 29 g carbohydrate, 0 fiber, 3 g protein. **Diabetic Exchanges:** 1 fruit, 1 fat-free milk.

Tasty Toast Strips

Verna Eaton, Woden, Illinois

Sprinkled with cinnamon and sugar, these yummy munchies come together in only 15 minutes for a busy-morning breakfast or speedy snack. I've shared the recipe with parents of young children, and even adults enjoy it.

2 tablespoons sugar
2 tablespoons brown sugar
1 teaspoon ground cinnamon
1/2 teaspoon ground nutmeg
1/4 cup butter, melted
3 bread slices

In a shallow bowl, combine the sugars, cinnamon and nutmeg. Place butter in another shallow bowl. Cut each slice of bread into four strips. Dip both sides in butter, then sprinkle with sugar mixture. Place on an ungreased baking sheet. Bake at 350° for 5-7 minutes or until golden brown. **Yield:** 1 dozen.

Fudgy Banana Muffins

Kristin Wagner, Spokane, Washington

We love the combination of chocolate and bananas. When I was out of chocolate chips, I made these moist muffins with chunks of candy bars instead. They were a hit!

1-1/4 cups all-purpose flour
1 cup whole wheat flour
3/4 cup packed brown sugar
1-1/2 teaspoons baking powder
1 teaspoon baking soda
1/4 teaspoon salt
3 medium ripe bananas, mashed
1-1/4 cups milk
1 egg
1 tablespoon vegetable oil
2 teaspoons vanilla extract
6 milk chocolate candy bars (1.55 ounces *each*)

In a mixing bowl, combine the flours, brown sugar, baking powder, baking soda and salt. In another bowl, combine bananas, milk, egg, oil and vanilla; stir into dry ingredients just until moistened.

Fill greased or paper-lined muffin cups one-third full. Break each candy bar into 12 pieces; place two pieces in each muffin cup. Top with remaining batter. Chop remaining candy bar pieces; sprinkle over batter. Bake at 400° for 15 minutes or until muffins test done. Cool for 5 minutes before removing from pans to wire racks. **Yield:** 1-1/2 dozen.

Fudgy Banana Muffins

Chocolate French Toast

Chocolate French Toast

Pat Habiger, Spearville, Kansas

With the yummy chocolate layer in this toast, you might be tempted to serve it for dessert instead of breakfast!

   3 eggs
   1 cup milk
   1 teaspoon sugar
   1 teaspoon vanilla extract
1/4 teaspoon salt
  12 slices day-old bread, crusts removed
   3 milk chocolate candy bars (1.55 ounces each), halved
   2 tablespoons butter
Confectioners' sugar

In a bowl, beat eggs, milk, sugar, vanilla and salt. Pour half into an ungreased 13-in. x 9-in. x 2-in. baking dish. Arrange six slices of bread in a single layer over egg mixture. Place one piece of chocolate in the center of each piece of bread. Top with remaining bread; pour remaining egg mixture over all. Let stand for 5 minutes.

In a large nonstick skillet, melt butter over medium heat. Fry sandwiches until golden brown on both sides. Dust with confectioners' sugar. Cut sandwiches diagonally; serve warm. **Yield:** 6 servings.

Editor's Note: Six 1-ounce squares of bittersweet or semisweet chocolate may be substituted for the milk chocolate candy bars. Heat squares in the microwave for 10 seconds before cutting into smaller pieces to place on the bread.

Four-Fruit Smoothie

(Pictured on page 76)

Kathleen Tribble, Santa Ynez, California

Cool and creamy, these fruit-filled drinks are fast to fix. All they require is cutting a banana and then processing the ingredients in a blender.

   1 cup orange juice
   1 package (10 ounces) frozen sweetened raspberries, partially thawed
   1 cup frozen unsweetened strawberries
   1 medium ripe banana, cut into chunks
   6 ice cubes
   1 to 2 tablespoons sugar
   4 orange wedges, optional

In a blender, combine the first six ingredients. Cover and process until smooth. Pour into chilled glasses. Garnish each smoothie with an orange wedge if desired. **Yield:** 4 cups.

Orange Fruit Baskets

(Pictured on page 76)

Our Test Kitchen staff carved these kid-pleasing containers from oranges, then added plenty of fresh fruit inside and a cute "flower" garnish on top.

    10 large navel oranges
     1 kiwifruit, peeled, sliced and quartered
    3/4 cup fresh blueberries
    3/4 cup sliced fresh strawberries
    3/4 cup halved green grapes
    3/4 cup halved red grapes
Additional red grapes and blueberries, optional

Peel and section two oranges; set aside. Make baskets from the remaining oranges as follows: For the handle, score a 1/2-in.-wide strip over the top of each orange. Score the peel from the base of the handle on one side to the opposite side. Cut along the scored lines with a paring knife and remove the peel. Repeat on other side.

Using a paring or grapefruit knife and spoon, scoop out the pulp from under the handle and inside of each basket. Combine the kiwi, berries and grapes and reserved orange segments; spoon into baskets. If desired, make a flower on top of each handle with grapes and blueberries as follows: Quarter six grapes; place three quarters on top of each handle with a blueberry in the center. **Yield:** 8 baskets.

Honey Bear French Toast

(Pictured on page 76)

Priscilla Weaver, Hagerstown, Maryland

In my family, French toast is welcome any time of day. This honey-sweetened recipe is especially delicious. For extra fun, shape the bread using a bear cookie cutter.

    18 slices Texas toast bread *or* 1-inch-thick
        slices Italian bread
    1/4 cup all-purpose flour
     1 tablespoon sugar
    1/8 teaspoon salt
     1 cup milk
     3 eggs, beaten
     3 tablespoons butter
    36 miniature chocolate chips
Warm honey

Using a 3-1/2-in. bear-shaped cookie cutter, cut bread into bear shapes. In a bowl, combine flour, sugar, salt, milk and eggs until smooth. Dip both sides of bread into egg mixture.

In a skillet, melt butter. Fry French toast for 2-3 minutes on each side or until golden brown. Transfer to serving plates; insert chocolate chips for eyes. Drizzle with honey. **Yield:** 18 slices.

Mallow Fruit Cups

Karen Coffman, Delphi, Indiana

To perk up plain fruit cocktail, I toss in a few of my family's favorite ingredients. The result is a pleasing side dish.

     1 can (15 ounces) fruit cocktail, drained
     1 medium tart apple, diced
    1/2 cup miniature marshmallows
    1/2 cup whipped topping

In a bowl, combine all ingredients. Cover and refrigerate until serving. **Yield:** 4-6 servings.

Pizza Pancakes

Maxine Smith, Owanka, South Dakota

I clipped this recipe from our local newspaper. The savory pancakes are best with warm pizza sauce.

     2 cups biscuit/baking mix
     2 teaspoons Italian seasoning
     2 eggs
     1 cup milk
    1/2 cup shredded part-skim mozzarella cheese
    1/2 cup chopped pepperoni
    1/2 cup chopped plum tomatoes
    1/4 cup chopped green pepper
     1 can (8 ounces) pizza sauce, warmed

In a large bowl, combine mix and seasoning. Combine eggs and milk; stir into dry ingredients just until moistened. Fold in cheese, pepperoni, tomatoes and pepper.

Pour batter by 1/4 cupfuls onto a lightly greased hot griddle. Turn when bubbles form on top; cook until the second side is golden brown. Serve with pizza sauce. **Yield:** 14 pancakes.

Pizza Pancakes

French Toast Fingers

French Toast Fingers

Mavis Diment, Marcus, Iowa

These scrumptious toast strips are filled with strawberry preserves and sprinkled with confectioners' sugar. They're not only a hit with kids, they're also great for buffets.

 Uses less fat, sugar or salt. Includes Nutrition Facts and Diabetic Exchanges.

- 2 eggs
- 1/4 cup milk
- 1/4 teaspoon salt
- 1/2 cup strawberry preserves
- 8 slices day-old white bread
- Confectioners' sugar, optional

In a small bowl, beat eggs, milk and salt; set aside. Spread preserves on four slices of bread; top with the remaining bread. Trim crusts; cut each sandwich into three strips. Dip both sides in egg mixture. Cook on a lightly greased hot griddle for 2 minutes on each side or until golden brown. Dust with confectioners' sugar if desired. **Yield:** 4 servings.

Nutrition Facts: One serving of three strips (prepared with egg substitute, fat-free milk and sugar-free preserves and without confectioners' sugar) equals 235 calories, 4 g fat (0 saturated fat), 2 mg cholesterol, 500 mg sodium, 42 g carbohydrate, 0 fiber, 10 g protein. **Diabetic Exchanges:** 2 starch, 1 meat, 1/2 fruit.

Peanut Butter 'n' Jelly Mini Muffins

Vickie Barrow, Edenton, North Carolina

Children and adults alike snatch up these yummy miniature muffins. With a jelly center and peanut butter in the batter, they're a fun and easy way to start off the day.

- 1 cup all-purpose flour
- 1/3 cup packed brown sugar
- 1 teaspoon baking powder
- 1/2 teaspoon baking soda
- 1/4 teaspoon salt
- 2 eggs
- 1/2 cup vanilla yogurt
- 3 tablespoons creamy peanut butter
- 2 tablespoons vegetable oil
- 3 tablespoons strawberry *or* grape jelly

In a large bowl, combine the flour, brown sugar, baking powder, baking soda and salt. In a small mixing bowl, beat the eggs, yogurt, peanut butter and oil on low speed until smooth; stir into the dry ingredients just until moistened.

Fill greased or paper-lined miniature muffin cups half full. Top each with 1/4 teaspoon jelly and remaining batter. Bake at 400° for 10-12 minutes or until golden brown. Cool for 5 minutes before removing from pans to wire racks. **Yield:** 2-1/2 dozen.

Editor's Note: Muffins may be baked in regular-size muffin cups for 16-18 minutes; use 3/4 teaspoon jelly for each instead of 1/4 teaspoon. Recipe makes 10 muffins.

Santa Pancakes

Christmas will be extra-special with this merry breakfast from our Test Kitchen staff. They used cherries and whipped cream to transform pancakes into the jolly old elf himself!

- 2 cups biscuit/baking mix
- 1 teaspoon ground cinnamon
- 2 eggs, beaten
- 1 cup milk
- 1 teaspoon vanilla extract
- 2 medium bananas, sliced
- 18 semisweet chocolate chips

Santa Pancakes

1 can (21 ounces) cherry pie filling
Whipped cream in a can

In a large bowl, combine baking mix and cinnamon. Combine the eggs, milk and vanilla; stir into dry ingredients just until moistened. Pour batter by 1/4 cupfuls onto a greased hot griddle. Turn when bubbles form on top; cook until second side is golden brown.

Place pancakes on individual plates. For Santa's eyes, place two banana slices on each pancake; top with a chocolate chip. For ears, cut remaining banana slices in half; place on either side of pancake. For nose, remove nine cherries from pie filling; place one in the center of each pancake. Spoon 1/4 cup pie filling above pancake for hat. Use whipped cream to spray the beard, hat brim and pom-pom. **Yield:** 9 servings.

Sunrise Mini Pizzas

Breakfast Cookies

Louise Gangwish, Shelton, Nebraska

I tried this recipe when I was a 4-H leader. Before morning chores, the young members would grab some of these crisp cookies, which are full of bacon, cornflakes and raisins.

      1/2 cup butter, softened
      3/4 cup sugar
        1 egg
        1 cup all-purpose flour
      1/4 teaspoon baking soda
       10 bacon strips, cooked and crumbled
        2 cups cornflakes
      1/2 cup raisins

In a mixing bowl, cream butter and sugar. Beat in egg. Add flour and baking soda; mix well. Stir in bacon, cornflakes and raisins. Drop by rounded tablespoonfuls 2 in. apart onto ungreased baking sheets.

Bake at 350° for 15-18 minutes or until lightly browned. Cool for 2 minutes before removing to wire racks. Store in the refrigerator. **Yield:** 2 dozen.

Tater Surprise

Paula West, St. Louis, Missouri

If your kids like Tater Tots, they'll love this tasty skillet. You can prepare it with any breakfast meat you choose.

      2-1/2 cups frozen Tater Tots *or* cubed hash
              brown potatoes
          1 cup chopped fully cooked ham
        1/4 cup chopped onion
        1/4 cup chopped green pepper
          2 tablespoons vegetable oil
          4 eggs, beaten
Salt and pepper to taste

In a large skillet, cook potatoes, ham, onion and green pepper in oil over medium heat for 8-10 minutes or un-

til browned, stirring constantly. (If using Tater Tots, break apart with a spatula; mix well.) Add eggs; cook and stir until eggs are completely set. Season with salt and pepper. **Yield:** 4 servings.

Sunrise Mini Pizzas

Teresa Silver, Melba, Idaho

I hit on this idea when I was trying to create "something different" for breakfast. The little pizzas go together quickly and are ideal for hectic school mornings.

          8 to 10 eggs
          3 tablespoons milk
Salt and pepper to taste
          1 tablespoon butter
         10 frozen white dinner rolls, thawed
         10 bacon strips, cooked and crumbled
          2 cups (8 ounces) shredded cheddar cheese

In a bowl, beat the eggs. Add milk, salt and pepper. Melt butter in a skillet; add the egg mixture. Cook and stir over medium heat until the eggs are set. Remove from the heat and set aside.

Roll each dinner roll into a 5-in. circle. Place on greased baking sheets. Spoon egg mixture evenly over crusts. Sprinkle with bacon and cheese. Bake at 350° for 15 minutes or until the cheese is melted. **Yield:** 10 pizzas.

Pizza Ideas

Try experimenting with different toppings when making your Sunrise Mini Pizzas (on this page). For example, add cooked sausage, peppers, onion, pepperoni or mushrooms.

Big Pine French Toast

Big Pine French Toast

Jan McCormick, Rosemount, Minnesota

Branch out with this tree-shaped toast that always gets smiles. Made with eggnog, it's a festive breakfast treat for the Christmas season.

    2 cups eggnog
    8 slices day-old bread
    8 pork sausage links
Green colored sugar
Confectioners' sugar
    4 orange slices and fresh herbs, optional

Pour eggnog into a shallow bowl; dip both sides of bread in eggnog. In a nonstick skillet, cook bread over medium heat for 2 minutes on each side or until golden brown. Meanwhile, in another skillet, brown the sausage.

Cut French toast diagonally; place four slices, overlapping slightly, on each serving plate for the tree. Place two sausages at the bottom for the trunk. Sprinkle with sugars. If desired, add an orange slice for the sun and herbs for grass. **Yield:** 4 servings.

Editor's Note: This recipe was tested with commercially prepared eggnog.

Chocolate Chip Pancakes

LeeAnn Hansen, Kaysville, Utah

What better way to give pancakes kid-appeal than by adding chocolate chips? This is a great breakfast for special days, but it's also fast enough to fit into busy mornings.

    2 cups all-purpose flour
    1/4 cup sugar
    2 tablespoons baking powder
    1 teaspoon salt
    2 eggs
 1-1/2 cups milk
    1/4 cup vegetable oil
    1/2 cup miniature chocolate chips
CINNAMON HONEY SYRUP:
    1 cup honey
    1/2 cup butter, cubed
    1 to 2 teaspoons ground cinnamon

In a bowl, combine the flour, sugar, baking powder and salt. Combine eggs, milk and oil; add to dry ingredients and mix well. Stir in chocolate chips. Pour the batter by 1/4 cupfuls onto a lightly greased hot griddle. Turn when bubbles form on top; cook until second side is golden brown. Keep warm.

Combine the ingredients for the syrup in a 2-cup microwave-safe bowl. Microwave, uncovered, on high until the butter is melted and the syrup is hot, stirring occasionally. Serve the syrup with the pancakes. **Yield:** 6 servings.

Honey Chip Granola Bars

RosAnna Troyer, Millersburg, Ohio

I first sampled these not-too-sweet treats at my mother-in-law's house. The marshmallow, honey and peanut butter mixture is delicious over the crunchy cereal, oats and nuts. Plus, the recipe makes a big batch.

    1/4 cup butter
    1/4 cup vegetable oil
 1-1/2 pounds miniature marshmallows
    1/4 cup honey
    1/4 cup peanut butter
    5 cups old-fashioned oats
 4-1/2 cups crisp rice cereal
    1 cup graham cracker crumbs (about 16 squares)
    1 cup flaked coconut
    1 cup crushed peanuts
    1/2 cup miniature chocolate chips

In a large saucepan, combine the butter, oil and marshmallows. Cook and stir over low heat until mixture is melted and smooth. Remove from the heat; stir in honey and peanut butter.

Combine the oats, cereal, cracker crumbs, coconut and peanuts. Add to the marshmallow mixture; mix well. Press into a greased 15-in. x 10-in. x 1-in. pan. Cool for 10-15 minutes. Sprinkle with chips and gently press into top. Cool completely. Cut into bars. **Yield:** about 4 dozen.

Editor's Note: Reduced-fat or generic brands of peanut butter are not recommended for this recipe.

Fruity Oatmeal
Brunch Punch
Peanut Butter Syrup

Fruity Oatmeal

Sarah Hunt, Everett, Washington

I never liked oatmeal until my mom found this yummy combination of uncooked oats and fresh fruit. Now I often make some myself for breakfast or as an afternoon snack.

1/3 cup old-fashioned oats
1 teaspoon oat bran
1/3 cup diced unpeeled tart apple
1 medium firm banana, diced
1/4 cup halved seedless grapes
2 tablespoons raisins
1 tablespoon sliced almonds
Milk *or* yogurt, optional

Toss the first seven ingredients; divide between two bowls. Top with milk or yogurt if desired. Serve immediately. **Yield:** 2 servings.

Peanut Butter Syrup

Janice Nightingale, Cedar Rapids, Iowa

We think this is the perfect topping for pancakes. It's thick, peanutty and can quickly be reheated in the microwave.

1/2 cup maple syrup
1/4 cup peanut butter
Waffles, pancakes *or* French toast

In a saucepan over low heat, heat syrup and peanut butter until peanut butter is melted. Stir until smooth. Serve warm over waffles, pancakes or French toast. **Yield:** about 2/3 cup.

Brunch Punch

Rosa Griffith, Christiansburg, Virginia

Youngsters love the sweet, tropical taste of this bright-colored beverage. It's so easy to make, you can stir some up just about anytime. The recipe requires only four basic ingredients.

2 cans (46 ounces *each*) tropical
punch-flavored soft drink
1 cup pineapple juice
3/4 cup lemonade concentrate
1 can (12 ounces) ginger ale, chilled

In a punch bowl or large container, combine the punch-flavored soft drink, pineapple juice and lemonade concentrate. Cover and refrigerate. Stir in ginger ale just before serving. **Yield:** about 3 quarts.

Coffee Cake Mix (p. 9

Chapter 7

Morning Mixes

These homemade blends for coffee cake, oatmeal and more are so easy to make, you'll never want store-bought mixes again!

Hot Cocoa Mix

Hot Cocoa Mix

Ruby Gibson, Newton, North Carolina

I first enjoyed this sweet treat during a camping trip in the mountains. A brimming mug was a wonderful way to warm up on crisp mornings.

6-2/3 cups nonfat dry milk powder
    1 cup instant chocolate drink mix
    1 package (5 ounces) cook-and-serve chocolate pudding mix
  1/2 cup confectioners' sugar
  1/2 cup powdered nondairy creamer
  1/2 cup baking cocoa
ADDITIONAL INGREDIENTS:
    1 cup boiling water
Miniature marshmallows, optional

In a bowl, combine the first six ingredients. Store in an airtight container in a cool dry place for up to 3 months. **Yield:** 21 batches (about 7 cups total).

    To prepare hot cocoa: Dissolve 1/3 cup cocoa mix in boiling water. Top with miniature marshmallows if desired. **Yield:** 1 serving per batch.

Raisin Oatmeal Mix

Robert Caummisar, Grayson, Kentucky

We love the flavor of this cinnamon oatmeal at our house. Thanks to the convenient mix, all we have to do is zap a bowl for a few minutes in the microwave.

    6 cups quick-cooking oats
  1/2 cup raisins
  1/2 cup chopped dried apples *or* bananas
  1/4 cup sugar
  1/4 cup packed brown sugar

    1 tablespoon ground cinnamon
    1 teaspoon salt
ADDITIONAL INGREDIENT FOR OATMEAL:
  3/4 cup water

In a bowl, combine the first seven ingredients. Store in an airtight container for up to 1 month. **Yield:** 14 batches (about 7 cups total).

    To prepare oatmeal: In a deep microwave-safe bowl, combine 1/2 cup oatmeal mix and the water. Microwave, uncovered, on high for 1 minute; stir. Cook 30-60 seconds longer or until bubbly. Let stand 1-2 minutes. **Yield:** 1 serving per batch.

    Editor's Note: This recipe was tested with an 850-watt microwave.

Whole-Grain Waffle Mix

Michelle Sheldon, Edmond, Oklahoma

My mother-in-law shared the recipe for this hearty blend. Just add a few ingredients to the mix, and you'll have golden, homemade waffles in minutes.

    4 cups whole wheat flour
    2 cups all-purpose flour
    1 cup toasted wheat germ
    1 cup toasted oat bran
    1 cup buttermilk blend powder
    3 tablespoons baking powder
    2 teaspoons baking soda
    1 teaspoon salt
ADDITIONAL INGREDIENTS:
    2 eggs
    1 cup water

Whole-Grain Waffle Mix

2 tablespoons vegetable oil
2 tablespoons honey

In a large bowl, combine the first eight ingredients. Store in an airtight container in the refrigerator for up to 6 months. **Yield:** 8-1/2 cups mix (about 4 batches).

To prepare waffles: Place 2 cups waffle mix in a bowl. Combine eggs, water, oil and honey; stir into waffle mix just until moistened. Bake in a preheated waffle iron according to manufacturer's directions until golden brown. **Yield:** 5 waffles (about 6 inches) per batch.

Editor's Note: Look for buttermilk blend powder next to the powdered milk in your grocery store.

Oatmeal Spice Mix

Marcy Waldrop, Deer Park, Texas

My daughters like packaged, flavored oatmeal for breakfast. But because store-bought oatmeal can be pricey, I experimented to create my own spice mix. The girls think it's even better than the purchased variety.

1/2 cup powdered nondairy creamer
1/2 cup confectioners' sugar
1/3 cup packed brown sugar
1 teaspoon salt
1/2 teaspoon ground cinnamon
1/4 teaspoon pumpkin pie spice
1/4 teaspoon ground nutmeg
ADDITIONAL INGREDIENTS (for each batch):
2/3 cup quick-cooking oats
1/3 to 1/2 cup boiling water
Brown sugar, optional

In a bowl, combine the first seven ingredients; mix well. Store in an airtight container in a cool dry place for up to 6 months. **Yield:** 9 batches (about 1 cup total).

To prepare oatmeal: In a bowl, combine oats and 2 tablespoons oatmeal spice mix. Add enough boiling water until oatmeal is desired consistency. Sprinkle with brown sugar if desired. **Yield:** 1 serving.

Cherry-Nut Muffin Mix

Marianne Clarke, Crystal Lake, Illinois

This twice-as-nice muffin recipe has a "bonus"—a sweetened and cardamon-spiced butter. That three-ingredient spread makes the perfect topping for these golden muffins dotted with dried cherries and walnuts.

2 cups all-purpose flour
1 cup sugar
1 teaspoon baking soda
1 teaspoon ground cardamom
1/2 to 1 teaspoon ground cloves
1/2 cup dried cherries *or* cranberries
1/2 cup chopped walnuts

Cherry-Nut Muffin Mix

ADDITIONAL INGREDIENTS:
1 cup buttermilk
1 egg
1/2 cup butter, melted
CARDAMOM BUTTER:
1/2 cup butter, softened
1/4 cup confectioners' sugar
1 teaspoon ground cardamom

In a small bowl, combine the flour, sugar and baking soda. In a 1-qt. glass container, layer the flour mixture, cardamom, cloves, cherries and walnuts, packing well between each layer. Cover and store in a cool dry place for up to 6 months. **Yield:** 1 batch (about 4 cups total).

To prepare muffins: Place mix in a large bowl. Combine the buttermilk, egg and butter; stir into mix just until moistened. Fill greased or paper-lined muffin cups three-fourths full. Bake at 400° for 20-25 minutes or until a toothpick comes out clean. Cool for 5 minutes before removing from pans to wire racks.

In a small mixing bowl, cream the butter, confectioners' sugar and cardamom until smooth. Store in an airtight container in the refrigerator. Soften just before serving with the muffins. **Yield:** 14 muffins (about 3/4 cup butter).

Merry Mix

For a quick gift at Christmastime, layer the dry ingredients in Cherry-Nut Muffin Mix (on this page) in a jar. Then tie on the preparation directions with a festive holiday ribbon.

Ham 'n' Swiss Pie Mix

Ham 'n' Swiss Pie Mix

Martha Warner, Lacombe, Alberta

I always have a batch of this in the cupboard so I can easily whip up a savory pie when I have leftover ham. Try using this blend in recipes that call for biscuit mix, too.

```
4-1/2  cups all-purpose flour
    2  tablespoons plus 1-1/2 teaspoons baking
       powder
1-1/2  teaspoons salt
    1  cup shortening
```
ADDITIONAL INGREDIENTS (for each pie):
```
    2  cups diced fully cooked ham
    1  cup (4 ounces) shredded Swiss cheese
    2  green onions, chopped
    3  eggs
1-1/2  cups milk
  1/4  teaspoon ground mustard
```
Dash pepper

In a large bowl, combine flour, baking powder and salt. Cut in shortening until crumbly. Store in an airtight container in a cool dry place for up to 6 months. **Yield:** 6 batches (about 6 cups mix).

To prepare pie: In a bowl, combine the ham, cheese and onions. Transfer to a greased 9-in. pie plate. In a mixing bowl, combine the eggs, milk, mustard, pepper and 1 cup mix; beat just until blended. Pour over ham mixture. Bake at 400° for 30-35 minutes or until a knife inserted near the center comes out clean. Let stand for 10 minutes before cutting. **Yield:** 6 servings.

Apple-Cinnamon Oatmeal Mix

Lynne Van Wagenen, Salt Lake City, Utah

Oatmeal is a breakfast staple at our house. We used to keep the pantry stocked with flavored mixes from the store, but we think this homemade version is even better. Feel free to substitute raisins or other dried fruit for the apples.

✓ **Uses less fat, sugar or salt. Includes Nutrition Facts and Diabetic Exchanges.**

```
    6  cups quick-cooking oats
1-1/3  cups nonfat dry milk powder
    1  cup dried apples, diced
  1/4  cup sugar
  1/4  cup packed brown sugar
    1  tablespoon ground cinnamon
    1  teaspoon salt
  1/4  teaspoon ground cloves
```
ADDITIONAL INGREDIENT (for each serving):
```
  1/2  cup water
```

In a large bowl, combine the first eight ingredients. Store in an airtight container in a cool dry place for up to 6 months. **Yield:** 8 cups total.

To prepare oatmeal: Shake the mix well. In a saucepan, bring the water to a boil; slowly stir in 1/2 cup mix. Cook and stir over medium heat for 1 minute. Remove from the heat. Cover and let stand for 1 minute or until the oatmeal reaches the desired consistency. **Yield:** 1 serving.

Nutrition Facts: One serving equals 176 calories, 2 g fat (trace saturated fat), 1 mg cholesterol, 185 mg sodium, 33 g carbohydrate, 4 g fiber, 7 g protein. **Diabetic Exchange:** 2 starch.

Spiced Tea Mix

Julie Dvornicky, Broadview Heights, Ohio

This was my grandmother's favorite tea mix. It's perfect to keep on hand for drop-in guests, and it can be served either hot or as iced tea.

```
    8  cups sweetened lemonade mix
    1  cup orange breakfast drink mix
  3/4  cup sugar
  1/2  cup unsweetened instant tea
    1  teaspoon ground nutmeg
  1/2  teaspoon ground cinnamon
  1/4  teaspoon ground cloves
```

Spiced Tea Mix

In a large bowl, combine all ingredients; mix well. Store in an airtight container in a cool dry place for up to 6 months. **Yield:** about 9 cups total.

To prepare 1 cup hot tea: Dissolve 2 tablespoons of tea mix in 1 cup of boiling water; stir well. **Yield:** 1 serving.

To prepare 1 gallon iced tea: Dissolve 2 cups of tea mix in 1 gallon of water; stir well. Serve over ice. **Yield:** 16 servings.

Cranberry Muffin Mix

Ruth Andrewson, Leavenworth, Washington

Muffins are always popular for breakfast, and this time-saving recipe gives you fresh-baked, homemade ones in a flash. The colorful cranberries make these goodies nice to serve at Christmastime, too.

  8-1/4 **cups all-purpose flour**
     3 **cups sugar**
   1/3 **cup baking powder**
     1 **tablespoon salt**
     1 **cup shortening**
ADDITIONAL INGREDIENTS:
     1 **egg**
     1 **cup evaporated milk**
     1 **tablespoon butter, melted**
     1 **cup fresh *or* frozen cranberries**

In a large bowl, combine the flour, sugar, baking powder and salt. Cut in shortening until the mixture resembles coarse crumbs. Store in an airtight container in a cool dry place for up to 6 months. **Yield:** about 4 batches (11-1/2 cups total).

To prepare muffins: Place 2-3/4 cups muffin mix in a bowl. Combine the egg, milk and butter; stir into mix just until moistened. Fold in cranberries. Fill greased or paper-lined muffin cups three-fourths full. Bake at 400° for 15-18 minutes or until a toothpick comes out clean. Cool for 5 minutes before removing from pan to a wire rack. Serve warm. **Yield:** 1 dozen.

Editor's Note: Contents of muffin mix may settle during storage. When preparing recipe, spoon mix into measuring cup.

Cappuccino Mix

Lois Britton, Selma, Alabama

For a quick-and-easy cappuccino, this simple mix can't be beat. Pair a steaming cup with your favorite scone or roll.

     1 **cup powdered nondairy creamer**
     1 **cup instant chocolate drink mix**
   2/3 **cup instant coffee granules**
   1/2 **cup sugar**
   1/2 **teaspoon ground cinnamon**
   1/4 **teaspoon ground nutmeg**

Homemade Pancake Mix

Combine all ingredients; mix well. Store in an airtight container. To serve, add 3 tablespoons mix to 3/4 cup boiling water; stir. **Yield:** 16 servings (3 cups mix).

Homemade Pancake Mix

Wendy Mink, Huntington, Indiana

Whole wheat flour adds flavor to these from-scratch flapjacks. My family likes the blueberry-banana variation best.

     4 **cups all-purpose flour**
     2 **cups whole wheat flour**
   2/3 **cup sugar**
     2 **tablespoons baking powder**
     1 **tablespoon baking soda**
ADDITIONAL INGREDIENTS FOR PANCAKES:
     1 **egg**
   3/4 **cup milk**
ADDITIONAL INGREDIENTS FOR BLUEBERRY BANANA PANCAKES:
     1 **egg**
   3/4 **cup milk**
     1 **medium ripe banana, mashed**
   3/4 **cup blueberries**

In a bowl, combine the first five ingredients. Store in an airtight container in a cool dry place for up to 6 months. **Yield:** 6-7 batches of pancakes (about 6-3/4 cups total).

To prepare pancakes: In a bowl, combine egg and milk. Whisk in 1 cup mix. Pour batter by 1/4 cupfuls onto a lightly greased hot griddle; turn when bubbles form on top of pancakes. Cook until second side is golden brown. **Yield:** about 6 pancakes per batch.

To prepare blueberry banana pancakes: In a bowl, combine egg, milk and banana. Whisk in 1 cup mix. Fold in blueberries. Cook as directed above. **Yield:** about 8 pancakes per batch.

Cake Doughnut Mix

Diane Terry, Queensburg, New York

I rely on this nicely spiced combination of ingredients to prepare delicious doughnuts any time we like. They're terrific served warm with hot coffee or cold milk.

4-1/2 cups all-purpose flour
    1 cup nonfat dry milk powder
    1 cup sugar
    2 tablespoons baking powder
1-1/2 teaspoons salt
    1 teaspoon ground cinnamon
    1 teaspoon ground nutmeg
1-1/2 cups shortening
ADDITIONAL INGREDIENTS (for each batch of doughnuts):
    2 eggs
  1/4 cup plus 1 tablespoon milk
    2 teaspoons vanilla extract
Oil for deep-fat frying
Confectioners' sugar, optional

In a large bowl, combine the flour, milk powder, sugar, baking powder, salt, cinnamon and nutmeg; cut in shortening until crumbly. Store in an airtight container in a cool dry place for up to 6 months. **Yield:** 2 batches (about 9 cups total).

To prepare doughnuts: Place 4-1/2 cups doughnut mix in a large bowl. Combine eggs, milk and vanilla; stir into doughnut mix just until moistened. Turn dough onto a floured surface; knead 15-20 times. Pat dough out to 1/2-in. thickness. Cut with a floured 3-in. doughnut cutter.

In an electric skillet or deep-fat fryer, heat oil to 375°. Fry a few doughnuts at a time, until golden brown, about 1-1/2 minutes on each side. Drain on paper towels. Dust with confectioners' sugar if desired. Serve warm. **Yield:** about 1 dozen.

Editor's Note: Contents of doughnut mix may settle during storage. When preparing recipe, spoon mix into measuring cup.

Poppy Seed Bread Mix

Laurie Marini, Newport, North Carolina

I'm always on the lookout for recipes that are quick, easy and use ingredients I normally have in my kitchen. This simple loaf fills the bill! It's delicious by itself or spread with cream cheese or jam.

  10 cups all-purpose flour
    4 cups sugar
    1 cup poppy seeds
  1/4 cup plus 2 teaspoons baking powder
    4 teaspoons salt
ADDITIONAL INGREDIENTS:
    1 egg
1-1/4 cups milk
  1/3 cup vegetable oil
    1 teaspoon vanilla extract

In a large bowl, combine the first five ingredients; mix well. Store in an airtight container in a cool dry place for up to 6 months. **Yield:** 4 batches (16 cups total).

To prepare one loaf: In a mixing bowl, combine the egg, milk, oil and vanilla. Add 4 cups bread mix; stir just until moistened. Pour into a greased 9-in. x 5-in. x 3-in. loaf pan. Bake at 350° for 55-60 minutes or until a toothpick inserted near the center comes out clean. Cool for 10 minutes; remove from pan to a wire rack. **Yield:** 1 loaf per batch.

Mint Cocoa Mix

LaVonne Hegland, St.Michael, Minnesota

I've mixed together this delectable blend many times during the Christmas season. But the mint flavor is so yummy, you'll want to keep some in your pantry year-round.

   1 package (30 ounces) instant chocolate
     drink mix
   1 package (25.6 ounces) nonfat dry milk
     powder
2-1/2 cups confectioners' sugar
   1 cup powdered nondairy creamer
  25 peppermint candies, crushed
ADDITIONAL INGREDIENT (for each serving):
   1 cup milk

In a large bowl, combine the first five ingredients; mix well. Store in an airtight container in a cool dry place for up to 6 months. **Yield:** 53 servings (17-2/3 cups total).

   To prepare hot drink: Warm milk; stir in 1/3 cup mix until dissolved. **Yield:** 1 serving.

Hearty Pancake Mix

Mavis Diment, Marcus, Iowa

Crushed cornflakes, wheat flour and old-fashioned oats create the multigrain mixture for these filling flapjacks. Served with butter and syrup, they're sure to get your family going in the morning.

   5 cups all-purpose flour
1-1/2 cups whole wheat flour
1-1/2 cups finely crushed cornflakes
   1 cup old-fashioned oats
   2 tablespoons sugar
   1 tablespoon baking powder
1-1/2 teaspoons baking soda
1-1/2 teaspoons salt
**ADDITIONAL INGREDIENTS (for each batch of
  pancakes):**
1-1/2 cups milk
   1 egg
   1 tablespoon vegetable oil

In a large bowl, combine the first eight ingredients; mix well. Store in an airtight container in a cool dry place for up to 6 months. **Yield:** 5 batches (7-1/2 cups total).

   To prepare pancakes: In a bowl, combine 1-1/2 cups mix, milk, egg and oil; whisk just until moistened. Pour batter by 1/4 cupfuls onto a lightly greased hot griddle.

Turn when bubbles form on top of pancakes; cook until second side is golden brown. **Yield:** 10 pancakes.

   Editor's Note: Contents of pancake mix may settle during storage. When preparing recipe, spoon mix into measuring cup.

Currant Scone Mix

Delores Hill, Helena, Montana

This delightful mix makes a pleasing treat any time of day. Leftover scones from breakfast are wonderful in the afternoon with a cup of tea.

   4 cups all-purpose flour
 2/3 cup sugar
 1/2 cup nonfat dry milk powder
   4 teaspoons baking powder
   1 teaspoon ground cinnamon
 1/2 teaspoon salt
 2/3 cup shortening
1-1/2 cups dried currants *or* raisins
ADDITIONAL INGREDIENTS (for each batch):
   1 egg, lightly beaten
 1/2 cup water

In a large bowl, combine the flour, sugar, milk powder, baking powder, cinnamon and salt. Cut in shortening until mixture resembles coarse crumbs. Add currants. Store in an airtight container in a cool dry place for up to 6 months. **Yield:** 2 batches (6 cups total).

   To prepare scones: In a large bowl, combine 3 cups mix, egg and water until moistened. Turn onto a lightly floured surface; knead 5-6 times. Transfer to a greased baking sheet and pat into a 9-in. circle. Cut into eight wedges (do not separate). Bake at 400° for 20-25 minutes or until golden brown. Serve warm. **Yield:** 8 scones.

Currant Scone Mix

Mexican Mocha Mix

Coffee Cake Mix

(Pictured on page 88)

Linnea Rein, Topeka, Kansas

Store this coffee-cake starter in your pantry, and you can whip up a last-minute treat in no time.

- 4 cups all-purpose flour
- 2 cups packed brown sugar
- 2/3 cup quick-cooking oats
- 1/3 cup buttermilk blend powder
- 2 teaspoons baking powder
- 2 teaspoons ground cinnamon
- 1 teaspoon salt
- 1/2 teaspoon ground nutmeg
- 1 cup shortening

TOPPING MIX:
- 1/2 cup graham cracker crumbs (about 8 squares)
- 1/2 cup chopped pecans
- 1/4 cup packed brown sugar
- 1/2 teaspoon ground cinnamon

ADDITIONAL INGREDIENTS:
- 2 eggs
- 1 cup water

In a large bowl, combine first eight ingredients; cut in shortening until crumbly. In a small bowl, combine topping ingredients. Store mixes in separate airtight containers in a cool dry place for up to 6 months. **Yield:** 2 batches (9 cups cake mix, 1-1/3 cups topping).

To prepare coffee cake: In a mixing bowl, combine eggs, water and 4-1/2 cups cake mix just until blended. Transfer to a greased 9-in. square baking pan. Sprinkle with 2/3 cup topping mix. Bake at 350° for 30-35 minutes or until a toothpick inserted near the center comes out clean. **Yield:** 1 cake (9 servings per batch).

Editor's Note: Look for buttermilk blend powder next the powdered milk in your grocery store.

Mexican Mocha Mix

Maria Regakis, Somerville, Massachusetts

With or without a cinnamon stick as a garnish, this blend of coffee and cocoa is a nicely spiced alternative to traditional hot chocolate. Rely on this convenient drink mix when you want a special hot beverage for overnight guests or holiday get-togethers.

✓ **Uses less fat, sugar or salt. Includes Nutrition Facts.**

- 3/4 cup baking cocoa
- 2/3 cup sugar
- 2/3 cup packed brown sugar
- 1/2 cup nonfat dry milk powder
- 1/3 cup instant coffee granules
- 3/4 teaspoon ground cinnamon
- 1/4 teaspoon ground allspice

ADDITIONAL INGREDIENTS (for each serving):
- 1 cup hot fat-free milk
- 1 cinnamon stick, optional

In a blender, combine the first seven ingredients; cover and process until the mixture forms a powder. Store in an airtight container. **Yield:** about 2-1/4 cups mix.

To prepare mocha beverage: In a mug, stir 3 tablespoons mocha mix with the hot milk until blended. Garnish the mocha drink with a cinnamon stick if desired. **Yield:** 1 serving.

Nutrition Facts: One serving equals 207 calories, 1 g fat (1 g saturated fat), 6 mg cholesterol, 172 mg sodium, 40 g carbohydrate, 2 g fiber, 12 g protein.

Chocolate-Cherry Coffee Mix

Jennifer Waters, Lubbock, Texas

I added cherry flavoring to a mocha drink mix to create this creamy coffee. Top it with sprinkles for extra fun.

- 3 cups sugar
- 2 cups confectioners' sugar
- 1-1/3 cups nondairy creamer
- 1-1/3 cups instant coffee granules
- 1 cup baking cocoa
- 1 envelope unsweetened cherry soft drink mix

ADDITIONAL INGREDIENTS (for each serving):
- 1 cup hot milk

Miniature marshmallows, optional
Holiday sprinkles, optional

In an airtight container, combine the first six ingredients. Store in a cool dry place for up to 2 months. **Yield:** 6 cups.

To prepare coffee: In a mug, dissolve 2 heaping tablespoons mix in the hot milk; stir well. Top with marshmallows and sprinkles if desired. **Yield:** 1 serving.

Butter Muffin Mix

Lois Stiteley, Sun City West, Arizona

Use this basic mix to make apricot muffins for breakfast or savory beef ones as a dinner accompaniment.

5-1/2 cups all-purpose flour
1/2 cup sugar
1/4 cup baking powder
1-1/2 teaspoons salt
3/4 cup cold butter
ADDITIONAL INGREDIENTS FOR APRICOT MUFFINS:
2 tablespoons sugar
1 egg
3/4 cup plus 1 tablespoon milk
1/4 teaspoon almond extract
1/4 cup chopped dried apricots
1/4 cup chopped slivered almonds, toasted
ADDITIONAL INGREDIENTS FOR BEEF AND ONION MUFFINS:
1 egg
3/4 cup plus 1 tablespoon milk
1 package (2-1/2 ounces) thinly sliced roast beef, finely chopped
1/4 cup chopped green onions

In a large bowl, combine the flour, sugar, baking powder and salt. Cut in butter until the mixture resembles coarse crumbs. Store in an airtight container in the refrigerator for up to 3 months. **Yield:** 3 batches (about 7 cups mix).

To prepare Apricot Muffins: In a large bowl, combine 2-1/3 cups muffin mix and sugar. Combine the egg, milk and almond extract; stir into the dry ingredients just until moistened. Fold in the dried apricots and toasted almonds. Fill greased or paper-lined muffin cups two-thirds full. Bake at 425° for 10-13 minutes or until a toothpick comes out clean. Cool muffins for 5 minutes before removing from pan to a wire rack. **Yield:** 1 dozen.

To prepare Beef and Onion Muffins: Place 2-1/3 cups muffin mix in a bowl. Combine the egg and milk; stir into the muffin mix just until moistened. Fold in the beef and green onions. Fill greased or paper-lined muffin cups two-thirds full. Bake at 425° for 10-13 minutes or until a toothpick comes out clean. Cool muffins for 5 minutes before removing from pan to a wire rack. **Yield:** 1 dozen.

Editor's Note: Contents of muffin mix may settle during storage. When preparing recipe, spoon mix into measuring cup.

Butter Muffin Mix

Banana Brunch Punch (p. 1

Chapter 8

Cooking for A Crowd

When you're serving breakfast or brunch to a bunch, rely on the large-yield recipes here. They're sure to go over big!

Brunch Strata

Arlene Butler, Ogden, Utah

Ham, zucchini, mushrooms and cheese make this morning bake flavorful and filling. If you'll be serving it at a buffet, bring copies of the recipe—everyone will want it!

      3 cups sliced fresh mushrooms
      3 cups chopped zucchini
      2 cups cubed fully cooked ham
  1-1/2 cups chopped onions
  1-1/2 cups chopped green peppers
      2 garlic cloves, minced
    1/3 cup vegetable oil
      2 packages (8 ounces *each*) cream cheese, softened
    1/2 cup half-and-half cream
     12 eggs
      4 cups cubed day-old bread
      3 cups (12 ounces) shredded cheddar cheese
      1 teaspoon salt
    1/2 teaspoon pepper

In a large skillet, saute the mushrooms, zucchini, ham, onions, green peppers and garlic in oil until vegetables are tender. Drain and pat dry; set aside.

In a large mixing bowl, beat the cream cheese and cream until smooth. Beat in eggs. Stir in the bread, cheese, salt, pepper and vegetable mixture.

Pour into two greased 11-in. x 7-in. x 2-in. baking dishes. Bake, uncovered, at 350° for 35-40 minutes or until a knife inserted near the center comes out clean. Let stand for 10 minutes before serving. **Yield:** 2 casseroles (8 servings each).

Sausage Bacon Bites

Pat Waymire, Yellow Springs, Ohio

These savory morsels sweetened with brown sugar are terrific with almost any egg dish for breakfast or brunch. Keep this recipe in mind for parties, too—you'll have fun finger foods that guests can just pop into their mouths.

    3/4 pound sliced bacon
      2 packages (8 ounces *each*) brown-and-serve sausage links
    1/2 cup plus 2 tablespoons packed brown sugar, *divided*

Cut bacon strips widthwise in half; cut sausage links in half. Wrap a piece of bacon around each piece of sausage. Place 1/2 cup brown sugar in a shallow bowl; roll sausages in sugar. Secure each with a toothpick. Place in a foil-lined 15-in. x 10-in. x 1-in. baking pan. Cover and refrigerate for 4 hours or overnight.

Sprinkle with 1 tablespoon brown sugar. Bake at 350° for 35-40 minutes or until bacon is crisp, turning once. Sprinkle with remaining brown sugar. **Yield:** about 3-1/2 dozen.

Warm Fruit Compote

Mary Ann Jonns, Midlothian, Illinois

With my slow cooker and just five ingredients, I can easily prepare this old-fashioned, comforting side dish. It's wonderful for the holiday season.

- 2 cans (29 ounces *each*) sliced peaches, drained
- 2 cans (29 ounces *each*) pear halves, drained and sliced
- 1 can (20 ounces) pineapple chunks, drained
- 1 can (15-1/4 ounces) apricot halves, drained and sliced
- 1 can (21 ounces) cherry pie filling

In a 5-qt. slow cooker, combine the peaches, pears, pineapple and apricots. Top with pie filling. Cover and cook on high for 2 hours or until heated through. Serve with a slotted spoon. **Yield:** 14-18 servings.

Peach Coffee Cake

Diana Krol, Nickerson, Kansas

This from-scratch coffee cake is a breeze to put together and makes a big pan. At Christmastime, I often replace the peach pie filling with cherry or strawberry.

- 1 cup butter, softened
- 1-3/4 cups sugar
- 4 eggs
- 3 cups all-purpose flour
- 1-1/2 teaspoons salt
- 1-1/2 teaspoons baking powder
- 1 can (21 ounces) peach pie filling
- ICING:
- 1-1/4 cups confectioners' sugar
- 1/2 teaspoon almond extract
- 3 to 4 tablespoons milk

Pretty Pink Punch

In a large mixing bowl, cream butter and sugar until light and fluffy. Add eggs, one at a time, beating well after each addition. Combine the flour, salt and baking powder; add to creamed mixture and beat just until combined.

Spread 3-3/4 cups batter into a greased 15-in. x 10-in. x 1-in. baking pan. Carefully spoon pie filling to within 1 in. of edges. Spoon remaining batter over filling. Bake at 350° for 20-25 minutes or until a toothpick inserted near center comes out clean (cover loosely with foil if edges brown too quickly). Cool on a wire rack.

In a small bowl, combine the icing ingredients. Drizzle over coffee cake. **Yield:** 16-20 servings.

Pretty Pink Punch

This colorful thirst-quencher from our Test Kitchen staff is deliciously tangy. For a special touch, follow the directions at the end of the recipe to make a flowery ice mold.

- 2 tablespoons sugar
- 3 cups cold water
- 2 bottles (64 ounces *each*) cranberry-raspberry drink, chilled
- 1 can (46 ounces) pineapple juice, chilled
- 1 can (12 ounces) frozen pink lemonade concentrate, thawed
- 1 liter ginger ale, chilled
- Decorative ice mold, optional

In a punch bowl, dissolve sugar in water. Add juices and lemonade; mix well. Stir in ginger ale. Top with an ice mold if desired. Serve immediately. **Yield:** 50 servings (7-1/2 quarts).

Editor's Note: To make the ice mold shown, arrange chemical-free edible flowers in a heart or ring mold. Carefully add enough water to partially cover flowers; freeze. Add enough water to cover flowers; freeze. Add water to desired depth; freeze.

Peach Coffee Cake

Breakfast Bake

Breakfast Bake

Kim Weaver, Olathe, Kansas

This fluffy egg dish sprinkled with bacon is not only terrific for breakfast, it's an easy-to-reheat meal for lunch or dinner, too. Feel free to make the two casseroles ahead of time and keep them in the freezer.

4-1/2 cups seasoned croutons
    2 cups (8 ounces) shredded cheddar cheese
    1 medium onion, chopped
1/4 cup chopped sweet red pepper
1/4 cup chopped green pepper
    1 jar (4-1/2 ounces) sliced mushrooms, drained
    8 eggs
    4 cups milk
    1 teaspoon salt
    1 teaspoon ground mustard
1/8 teaspoon pepper
    8 bacon strips, cooked and crumbled

Sprinkle croutons, cheese, onion, peppers and mushrooms into two greased 8-in. square baking dishes. In a bowl, combine the eggs, milk, salt, mustard and pepper. Slowly pour over vegetables. Sprinkle with bacon.

Cover and freeze the casseroles for up to 3 months. Or bake the casseroles, uncovered, at 350° for 45-50 minutes or until a knife inserted near the center comes out clean. Let stand for 10 minutes before cutting.

To use frozen casseroles: Completely thaw in the refrigerator for 24-36 hours. Remove from the refrigerator 30 minutes before baking. Bake, uncovered, at 350°

for 50-60 minutes or until a knife inserted near the center comes out clean. Let stand for 10 minutes before cutting. **Yield:** 2 casseroles (6-8 servings each).

Glazed Fruit Bowl

Christine Wilson, Sellersville, Pennsylvania

Summer favorites such as melon and berries combine in this quick medley. It's a great way to serve fruit to a group.

✓ **Uses less fat, sugar or salt. Includes Nutrition Facts and Diabetic Exchanges.**

    2 cans (20 ounces *each*) unsweetened pineapple chunks
    2 packages (3 ounces *each*) cook-and-serve vanilla pudding mix
2-1/2 cups orange juice
    1 small cantaloupe, cubed
3-1/2 cups cubed honeydew
    2 cups fresh strawberries, halved
    2 cups fresh blueberries
    2 cups seedless grapes
    2 medium firm bananas, sliced

Drain pineapple, reserving 1 cup juice; set pineapple aside. (Discard remaining juice or save for another use.) In a large saucepan, combine the pudding mix, pineapple juice and orange juice. Cook and stir over medium heat until mixture boils and thickens. Remove from the heat; cool.

In a large bowl, combine the pineapple, melon, berries, grapes and bananas. Drizzle with the pudding mixture. Refrigerate until serving. **Yield:** 25 servings.

Nutrition Facts: 3/4 cup (prepared with sugar-free

Glazed Fruit Bowl

pudding mix) equals 82 calories, trace fat (trace saturated fat), 0 cholesterol, 43 mg sodium, 20 g carbohydrate, 2 g fiber, 1 g protein. **Diabetic Exchange:** 1-1/2 fruit.

Three-Grain Muffins

Dorothy Collins, Winnsboro, Texas

This crowd-size recipe mixes oats, two breakfast cereals and buttermilk to create scrumptious, moist muffins. Serve them with jam or a cream cheese spread.

     2 cups quick-cooking oats
     2 cups crushed Shredded Wheat (about 4 large)
     2 cups All-Bran
     1 quart buttermilk
     1 cup boiling water
     1 cup vegetable oil
     4 eggs, beaten
 2-1/4 cups packed brown sugar
     5 cups all-purpose flour
     5 teaspoons baking soda
     1 teaspoon salt

In a large bowl, combine oats, Shredded Wheat and bran. Add buttermilk, water, oil and eggs; stir for 1 minute. Stir in sugar. Combine flour, baking soda and salt; add to the cereal mixture and stir well.

Fill greased or paper-lined muffin cups two-thirds full. Bake at 400° for 18-20 minutes or until a toothpick comes out clean. Cool for 10 minutes; remove from pans to wire racks. **Yield:** 4 dozen.

Editor's Note: Muffin batter can be stored in the refrigerator for up to 1 week.

Pancakes for a Crowd

Penelope Hamilton, Riverside, California

If you're ever in charge of fixing breakfast for 70 people or more, you'll want to pull out this tried-and-true recipe.

    40 cups all-purpose flour
     3 cups sugar
 1-1/2 cups baking powder
 1-1/2 cups baking soda
   3/4 cup salt
    28 eggs
     2 gallons milk
     1 gallon buttermilk
    64 ounces vegetable oil

In several large bowls, combine the flour, sugar, baking powder, baking soda and salt. Combine the eggs, milk, buttermilk and oil; stir into dry ingredients just until blended.

Three-Grain Muffins

Pour batter by 1/3 cupfuls onto a greased hot griddle. Turn when bubbles form on top; cook until second side is golden brown. **Yield:** 70-80 servings (5 gallons of batter).

Banana Brunch Punch

(Pictured on page 98)

Mary Anne McWhirter, Pearland, Texas

For a special occasion, it's nice to offer guests a flavorful fruit blend like this instead of ordinary orange juice.

     6 medium ripe bananas
     1 can (12 ounces) frozen orange juice concentrate, thawed
     1 can (6 ounces) frozen lemonade concentrate, thawed
     3 cups warm water, *divided*
     2 cups sugar, *divided*
     1 can (46 ounces) pineapple juice
     3 bottles (2 liters *each*) lemon-lime soda
Orange slices, optional

In a blender or food processor, blend bananas and concentrates until smooth. Remove half of the mixture and set aside. Add 1-1/2 cups warm water and 1 cup sugar to mixture in blender; blend until smooth. Place in a large freezer container. Repeat with remaining banana mixture, water and sugar; add to container. Cover and freeze until solid.

One hour before serving, take punch base out of freezer. Just before serving, place in a large punch bowl. Add pineapple juice and soda; stir until well blended. Garnish with orange slices if desired. **Yield:** 60-70 servings (10 quarts).

Cinnamon Focaccia

Page Alexander, Baldwin City, Kansas

A nutty cinnamon-sugar topping and a drizzle of glaze add sweetness to this lovely bread. It's a refreshing change of pace from the usual breakfast loaf or coffee cake.

> 6 to 6-1/2 cups all-purpose flour
> 2 packages (1/4 ounce *each*) active dry yeast
> 1 teaspoon salt
> 2 cups warm water (120° to 130°)
> 1/4 cup vegetable oil
> 1/4 cup butter, melted
> 1/3 cup sugar
> 1 teaspoon ground cinnamon
> 1/2 to 1 cup chopped nuts
> 1-1/2 cups confectioners' sugar
> 3 to 4 tablespoons half-and-half cream

In a mixing bowl, combine 2 cups flour, yeast and salt. Add water and oil; beat until smooth. Stir in enough remaining flour to form a soft dough. Turn onto a floured surface; knead until smooth and elastic, about 6-8 minutes. Place in a greased bowl, turning once to grease top. Cover and let rise in a warm place until doubled, about 1 hour.

Punch dough down. Turn onto a lightly floured surface; divide in half. Pat each portion flat. Cover and let stand for 10 minutes. Press dough into two greased 12-in. pizza pans. Prick top of dough with a fork. Brush with butter. Combine sugar and cinnamon; sprinkle over dough. Top with nuts. Let stand 10-15 minutes.

Bake at 350° for 25-30 minutes or until lightly browned. Remove from pans to wire racks. Combine confectioners' sugar and enough cream to achieve a glaze consistency; drizzle over warm bread. **Yield:** 2 round loaves.

Cinnamon Focaccia

Blueberry Mini Muffins

Blueberry Mini Muffins

Suzanne Fredette, Littleton, Massachusetts

These bite-size goodies are especially nice for morning potlucks. The recipe makes 7 dozen, and the small muffins leave plenty of room on your plate for all of the other foods you want to sample.

> 1 cup butter, softened
> 2 cups sugar
> 5 eggs
> 1 cup buttermilk
> 2 teaspoons vanilla extract
> 5 cups all-purpose flour
> 1 teaspoon baking soda
> 1 teaspoon baking powder
> 3/4 teaspoon salt
> 3 cups fresh *or* frozen blueberries
> Additional sugar, optional

In a mixing bowl, cream butter and sugar. Add eggs, buttermilk and vanilla; mix well. Combine flour, baking soda, baking powder and salt; stir into the creamed mixture just until moistened. Fold in blueberries (batter will be thick).

Fill greased or paper-lined miniature muffin cups with about a tablespoon of batter. Sprinkle with sugar if desired. Bake at 400° for 10-15 minutes or until a toothpick comes out clean. Cool for 5 minutes before removing from pan to a wire rack. **Yield:** 7 dozen.

Oven Scrambled Eggs

Terry Bringhurst, Berlin, New Jersey

Cooking for a youth camp during the summer, I grew accustomed to preparing large quantities of food. I altered a scrambled egg recipe shared by a previous cook, and the result was this easy-to-make version.

2	cups butter, melted
100	eggs, beaten
3	tablespoons salt
2-1/2	quarts milk

Divide butter among four 13-in. x 9-in. x 2-in. baking dishes. Combine eggs and salt; mix well. Gradually stir in milk. Pour evenly into baking dishes.

Bake, uncovered, at 350° for 10 minutes; stir. Bake 10-15 minutes more or until eggs are set. Serve immediately. **Yield:** 100 servings.

Warm-You-Up Sausage Quiche

Renae Moncur, Burley, Idaho

To remind my daughter of the snowy winter season in her home state, I planned a snowman-theme brunch while visiting her in California. This flavor-packed and cheesy quiche got a reception that was far from chilly!

1	pound bulk mild pork sausage
1/4	pound bulk hot pork sausage
12	eggs
2	cups (16 ounces) small-curd cottage cheese
3	cups (12 ounces) shredded Monterey Jack cheese
1	cup (4 ounces) shredded part-skim mozzarella cheese
1/2	cup all-purpose flour
1/2	cup butter, melted
1	teaspoon baking powder
2	cups sliced fresh mushrooms
3/4	cup finely chopped onion
1	can (4 ounces) chopped green chilies, drained

Grated Parmesan cheese, optional
Green and sweet red pepper strips, optional

In a large skillet over medium heat, cook sausage until no longer pink; drain. In a large mixing bowl, beat eggs, cheeses, flour, butter and baking powder. Stir in mushrooms, onion, chilies and sausage.

Transfer to two greased 9-in. round baking dishes (dishes will be full). Sprinkle with Parmesan cheese if desired. Bake at 375° for 33-38 minutes or until a knife inserted near the center comes out clean. Let stand for 10 minutes before cutting. Garnish with pepper strips if desired. **Yield:** 2 quiches (6-8 servings each).

Warm-You-Up Sausage Quiche

Special Cinnamon Rolls

Special Cinnamon Rolls

Brenda Deveau, Van Buren, Maine

You'll save a step when you prepare these irresistible yeast rolls because the dough doesn't require kneading.

- 2 packages (1/4 ounce *each*) active dry yeast
- 1/2 cup warm water (110° to 115°)
- 8 cups all-purpose flour
- 1 package (3.4 ounces) instant vanilla pudding mix
- 2 cups warm milk (110° to 115°)
- 2 eggs, lightly beaten
- 1/2 cup sugar
- 1/2 cup vegetable oil
- 2 teaspoons salt
- 1/4 cup butter, melted

FILLING:
- 1 cup packed brown sugar
- 2 teaspoons ground cinnamon
- 1 cup raisins
- 1 cup chopped walnuts

GLAZE:
- 1 cup confectioners' sugar
- 1 to 2 tablespoons milk
- 1/4 teaspoon vanilla extract

In a mixing bowl, dissolve yeast in water. Add next seven ingredients; mix well (do not knead). Place in a greased bowl; turn once to grease top. Cover and let rise in warm place until doubled, about 1 hour.

Punch down. Turn onto a lightly floured surface; divide in half. Roll each half into a 12-in. x 8-in. rectangle; brush with butter. Combine filling ingredients; spread over dough. Roll up from long side; seal seam.

Slice each roll into 12 rolls; place cut side down in two greased 13-in. x 9-in. x 2-in. baking pans. Cover and let rise until nearly doubled, 45 minutes.

Bake at 350° for 25-30 minutes or until golden brown. Combine glaze ingredients; drizzle over rolls. Cool in pans on wire tracks. **Yield:** 2 dozen.

Mixed Berry Pizza

Gretchen Widner, Sun City West, Arizona

For a delightfully different way to serve fruit, try this colorful pizza bursting with fresh berries.

✓ **Uses less fat, sugar or salt. Includes Nutrition Facts and Diabetic Exchanges.**

- 1 tube (8 ounces) refrigerated reduced-fat crescent rolls
- 11 ounces reduced-fat cream cheese
- 1/2 cup apricot preserves
- 2 tablespoons confectioners' sugar
- 2 cups sliced fresh strawberries
- 1 cup fresh blueberries
- 1 cup fresh raspberries

Unroll crescent roll dough and place in a 15-in. x 10-in. x 1-in. baking pan coated with nonstick spray. Press onto the bottom and 1 in. up the sides of pan to form a crust; seal seams and perforations. Bake at 375° for 8-10 minutes or until golden. Cool completely.

In a mixing bowl, beat cream cheese until smooth. Beat in preserves and confectioners' sugar; spread over crust. Cover and refrigerate for 1-2 hours. Just before serving, arrange berries on top. Cut into 20 pieces. **Yield:** 20 servings.

Nutrition Facts: One serving (1 piece) equals 110 calories, 5 g fat (2 g saturated fat), 9 mg cholesterol, 143 mg sodium, 15 g carbohydrate, 1 g fiber, 3 g protein. **Diabetic Exchanges:** 1 fruit, 1/2 starch.

Mixed Berry Pizza

Hash Brown Bake

Dorothy Byrom, Overland Park, Kansas

Every time I present this cheesy dish, it gets rave reviews. Using purchased hash browns speeds up the preparation.

      7 cups water
      2 packages (32 ounces *each*) frozen
         Southern-style hash brown potatoes
      2 packages (8 ounces *each*) cream cheese,
         softened
      4 eggs
      2 teaspoons minced chives
 1-1/4 teaspoons salt
    1/2 teaspoon pepper
    1/4 cup dry bread crumbs
    1/4 cup grated Parmesan cheese
      3 tablespoons butter, melted

In a Dutch oven, bring water and potatoes to a boil. Reduce heat; cover and simmer until potatoes are tender, about 12 minutes. Drain. Place potatoes in a mixing bowl; beat on low until mashed. Add cream cheese, eggs, chives, salt and pepper; mix well.

Divide potato mixture between two greased 2-qt. baking dishes. Combine bread crumbs, Parmesan cheese and butter; sprinkle over potatoes. Cover and refrigerate overnight.

Remove from the refrigerator 30 minutes before baking. Bake, uncovered, at 350° for 50-60 minutes or until top is browned and potatoes are heated through. **Yield:** 24 servings.

French Toast for 90

Kathleen Hall, Lakeview, Oregon

When I made this baked toast for our senior center, everyone was pleased. You can easily cut the recipe in half.

      9 unsliced loaves (1 pound *each*) day-old
         French bread
      9 dozen eggs
 2-1/2 gallons milk
      2 cups sugar
      1 cup vanilla extract
      2 tablespoons salt
      1 pound butter, melted
Confectioners' sugar

Slice bread into 3/4-in. pieces; arrange in 18 greased 13-in. x 9-in. x 2-in. baking dishes. Beat eggs; add milk, sugar, vanilla and salt. Mix well. Pour about 3 cups over bread in each pan. Cover and chill 8 hours or overnight.

Remove from refrigerator 30 minutes before baking. Brush with butter. Bake, uncovered, at 350° for 55-65 minutes or until a knife inserted near the center comes out clean. Let stand 5 minutes. Dust with confectioners' sugar. **Yield:** 90 servings (2 slices each).

Ham and Cheese Puff

Ham and Cheese Puff

Nina Clark, Wareham, Massachusetts

This recipe is a true winner for breakfast and even supper. People really go for the big chunks of ham and cheese.

      2 loaves (1 pound *each*) Italian bread, cut
         into 1-inch cubes
      6 cups cubed fully cooked ham
 1-1/2 pounds Monterey Jack *or* Muenster
         cheese, cubed
      1 medium onion, chopped
    1/4 cup butter
     16 eggs
      7 cups milk
    1/2 cup prepared mustard

Toss bread, ham and cheese; divide between two greased 13-in. x 9-in. x 2-in. baking dishes. In a skillet, saute onion in butter until tender; transfer to a bowl. Add eggs, milk and mustard; mix well. Pour over bread mixture. Cover and refrigerate overnight.

Remove from the refrigerator 30 minutes before baking. Bake, uncovered, at 350° for 55-65 minutes or until a knife inserted near the center comes out clean. Serve immediately. **Yield:** 24-30 servings.

Get Set for Guests

To save time, do the following the night before your brunch: Set the table, put out the serving dishes and utensils, prepare make-ahead foods and measure the coffee.

☀ General Recipe Index

This index lists every recipe by food category and/or major ingredient, so you can easily locate recipes to suit your needs.

Best of Country Breakfast & Brunch

Alphabetical Index

This index lists every recipe in alphabetical order so you can easily find your favorite recipes.